A GUIDE FOR WIDOWHOOD

A GUIDE FOR WIDOWHOOD

NAVIGATING THE FIRST THREE YEARS

LIFE STAGES FINANCIAL GUIDES

DONNA JEAN KENDRICK

HIGHLANDER
PRESS

A Guide for Widowhood. Second Edition ©2024, 2022 Donna Jean Kendrick

CHECKOUT DONNA'S BACKGROUND ON FINRA'S BROKERCHECK

Cetera Financial Specialists LLC, member FINRA/SIPC, is a registered representative offering securities. Advisory services are offered through Cetera Investment Advisers LLC. Cetera is under separate ownership from any other named entity. Sephton Financial, LLC and Cetera are not affiliated.

This communication is strictly intended for those residing in DC, DE, FL, GA, MA, MD, NJ, NY, PA, VA, VT, and WA.

ISBN: 978-1-956442-46-5
Ebook ISBN: 978-1-956442-47-2
Library of Congress Control Number: Applied For.

Published by Highlander Press
501 W. University Pkwy, Ste. B2
Baltimore, MD 21210

Original cover design: Lindsey Burda
Cover update: Hanne Broter
Author photo: Sarah Miller

Ordering Information: Special discounts are available on quantity purchases. **Contact: hello@donnajeankendrick.com** Grief Recovery Specialist®

To my dad, the late Phil Sephton, who taught me patience, work ethic, and humor and did all he could to ensure my education. When Greg passed, that education gave me confidence so I could stand on my own two feet.

My financial planning practice is named Sephton Financial after my dad…years after he had passed. He thought he was a blue-collar worker who would never have his "name on a door."
I made sure he did.

DISCLAIMER

CONTENTS

INTRODUCTION

If you received this book from a friend or a loved one, or you googled and found it on your own, that probably means you have entered the club you never wanted to join: widowhood. My heart is with you. Because if you're reading this book and have lost your spouse or partner, you've probably lost the love of your life. Or, maybe you bought this book to help someone you care deeply about so that you can learn and be a good resource for them. You want to help make sure they make the next right moves, at least regarding their finances. Either way, this book is here for you to help as a roadmap along this journey into widowhood.

   In the days, weeks, months, and years after a loss, there is so much upheaval in almost every aspect of your and your family's lives. I know the pain. I know the fog. I know the need to crawl and scratch until you can get control of your own life because everything feels like it's swirling. I know because in 2013, at age forty, I lost my husband of thirteen years, Gregory. The loss was sudden; he took his own life. And although I was educated, smart, organized, and financially savvy, I was emotionally crushed. I spent the next few years pulling myself together and raising my children, who were eight, eleven, and twelve at the time. After the first year or so, once I learned I could handle the centripetal force of life, I took a deep breath…literally…and in a breath, decided to recreate my career and make sure that I could help men and women in widowhood make the right financial decisions and feel empowered, smart, and in control.

I wrote this book to guide you. There are resources available to assist in organizing the early days, knowing that you are preoccupied with the thoughts and details that now invade your widowed brain. There are stories to help you come into equilibrium with the pain. There are examples and suggestions of how I work with my clients to help give you direction. There are choices to be made while you are in the darkness of grief; this book is an aide to managing the overwhelm. I wrote this book so you can have peace of mind, pride, and the ability to move forward with financial grace.

You may be wondering how to best use this book. Read it all at once or go chapter by chapter according to where you are in the widowhood process. If you need immediate guidance, skip the **Backstory** and **My Story** chapters and jump right into **Your First 24 Hours.** Many resources and checklists are available right in the chapters. More detailed versions with annotations are provided as photo pages nearby. The guides and checklists are also provided in the easily referenced Resource Section at the rear of the book. As my gift to you, the resources of this book are available for download and printout from their source page: www.donnakendrick.com.

Remember, there is no need to read this book all at once. If you have recently lost a spouse or partner, focus on the chapters in the **Year of Firsts.** There is also no need to make all your decisions at one time. I often hear those in widowhood saying that they felt like they were drinking from a firehose; everything came at them at once. They were overwhelmed and made decisions and choices during this chaos. I give you permission to say F-that. You are allowed to slow the roll. This is your journey to take control of. I am here for you in the pages. I am here for you if you need more; reach out for some reinforcement when needed: hello@donnajeankendrick.com.

STAGES OF FINANCIAL
DECISIONS IN WIDOWHOOD

HERE IS A FRAMEWORK OF HOW I HELP MY CLIENTS navigate the first few years of widowhood. I share this framework so that you have a point of reference for the education in the pages to come.

IMMEDIATE GOALS: THE YEAR OF THE FIRSTS

Immediate goals are the *Have To* goals. These are the goals that happen the day after the loss and carry through the first year or two. From making funeral plans, to finding life insurance policies, to digging through boxes of paperwork to figure out your spouse's group benefits. These are the immediate goals, and let me tell you, they are unfair. You are making big decisions when the world is spinning…but you have to, they are NOT optional. They are time sensitive. In further chapters, we will be providing checklists, video links, and downloadable resources to help keep you sane and moving forward.

TRANSITIONAL GOALS: YEAR TWO

Transitional goals are the *Need To* goals. These are goals that happen after you have experienced the "Year of the Firsts." These are the decisions that help set the direction of the next few years:

- Stay in our home, sell and buy new or maybe rent?
- Make an improvement to the home?
- How do I need to adjust my goals to my new financial reality?
- What do I need to do to ensure that I can afford to take care of myself and my children?
- Can I buy a new car, or should I fix our old one?
- How much do I need to start saving since retirement savings depends only on me right now?

Need To goals help you keep your sanity, give you direction and purpose, and help you feel in control as you continue making necessary decisions on your own.

LONG-TERM GOALS: YEARS THREE TO FIVE

Long-term goals are the *Want To* goals. These goals are for things like:

- What does retirement actually look like?
- What conversations do I need to have with my kids so they understand how financial aid works or how we pay for college?
- What kind of loans are available to me?

Long-term goals are an opportunity to soul search after you have had a few years of experience in navigating life alongside of grief. I often guide my clients who are many years out from their loss to take an inventory of these prompts:

- What do you *want* this next chapter of your life to look like?
- What value do you *want* to share with those around you?

Long-term goals might also include blending families. Life does move forward after loss and often love does too. Blending finances is an art form.

OUR PATH

- **Immediate goals**: The stuff you *Have To* get done. The nonnegotiable .
- **Transitional goals**: This is the new reality and how are we managing through it. What has to change so we can live our best life? These are the *Need To* goals.
- **Long-term goals**: About three to five years after loss, when you finally have your groove on. These are the *Want To* goals

Like the Tilt-a-Whirl on the Ocean City boardwalk in New Jersey, the world feels "spinny" after a loss. I hope I can slow the velocity of it all for you.

THE BACKSTORY

In 2000, Greg and I were newly married after having dated for just over three years. He was the son of a Philadelphia police officer, and I was the daughter of a Philadelphia firefighter. So let's say that if sharing the same Police and Fire Credit Union was an indication of a good fit, then we were perfect. We got married in March, the day after St. Patrick's Day. My good Irish Catholic married his little English Protestant. The jokes abounded, but we enjoyed it. Greg was so happy that we got married in the year 2000 because he figured he would never forget our anniversary. Being a statistics major, I respected his decision to make sure we were married in the new millennium.

At the time of our marriage, Greg worked for the United States government as a federal law enforcement officer. His career had already been a long one since he started with the agency as in intern back in college. He traveled a lot which was the part of the job that he loved, jet setting around the world, seeing different cultures, and helping make America a safer place. At the same time, I worked in a role as a financial forecaster for the pharmaceutical industry. We were making almost the same income. We were both ambitious and driven. I guess you'd call us yuppies, young urban professionals.

Our first house was a single family home in the suburbs of Philadelphia over the bridge in New Jersey, on a beautiful, wooded corner lot in a wonderful school district. The only downfall truly was the leaf pickup. Two city kids were not prepared for the nonstop mounds of leaves, mulch, and mush that our corner castle produced. We spent our Saturdays with leaf blowers, whirling their obnoxious white noise, pointed at a sea of laid out old king-sized bedsheets. I am still amazed that, by our early twenties, we had saved the funds for a down payment on our home, as well as the funds to pay for a majority of our wedding. We were able to afford our first house down payment of $40k in 1999, at such an early age, because we were both hard workers who knew the power of savings for both short-term and long-term goals. When we had a goal that we wanted to accomplish in a year or two, we took on overtime or a second job and saved that extra income towards that goal.

Like a good Irish Catholic family, we had our first baby, Connor, three months after our one-year anniversary. Our second child, Katie, our Irish twin, arrived twelve months later. My employer was not thrilled that I came back from my four-month maternity leave, after having Connor, pregnant again. I experienced severe morning sickness with both pregnancies, so my coworkers and I literally rolled my computer into the handicapped bathroom stall so I could work and have a place to vomit close by without having to sprint. Our family was blossoming, and I loved minute of it.

Soon after Katie's birth, life got very busy. Greg traveled more. My job was an hour commute from our home, and we racked up fines for overextending our daycare because I would get caught in traffic and be late for 6:00 p.m. pick up—fifty dollars for every half hour we were late! We simply had to regroup. We were emotionally, physically, and financially exhausted.

I did a financial triage of our budget, of our future savings, of the needs and cost of care for our kids, and our future educational goals for them. I decided to go part time. I said, "I," because sometimes in life you have to take a deep breath and take control. Greg was away from the house 70% of the month, so all aspects of parenting, finances, and homeownership were on me. So, I pulled the plug on working full-time during one of his trips to Washington, D.C. By moving to part-time employment, I was able to work at night. My employer was an international firm who welcomed someone working night hours on the east coast, that way I was interacting directly, in real time, with our New Zealand colleagues. This schedule helped Greg and I avoid the cost of daycare. Exhausting but *sooooooooooo* worth it. Full throttle!

Amazing change came to our life at that time when Greg got offered a long-term detail to Rome, Italy, a long-time goal of his. I packed up the kids and we followed him. The first assignment lasted about a year. As soon as we returned to the States, we added our son, James, aka Squish (because of the rolls of wonderful baby fat that stuck around for years), to our family. Within two years, we were back in Rome for a longer, more permanent stay.

Greg and I were squared away. We knew our budget, we knew our income, we knew our goals. We knew what we could and could not do financially. Moving to Rome was going to provide a wonderful opportunity for us because, without a mortgage, we would be able to save money towards all those things in life that might have been unattainable on one full-time income. We also knew that we'd be selling our beautiful starter home on the wooded corner lot. And because the market in real estate had gained value so much between 1999 and 2007, we made a significant profit on that home.

We took some advice from a good friend and got ourselves a financial advisor. Our young, new advisor, Mark, sat with us and created a plan. He made sure we had adequate insurance protection and identified some strengths in our current finances, as well as some future weaknesses that we hadn't foreseen. One of those weaknesses was that Greg would be retiring early because he was in law enforcement and officers were required to retire at age fifty-seven.

Mark brought to light that we would have to supplement his pay, and perhaps afford our health care costs, from age fifty-seven to at least age fifty-nine-and-a-half when Greg could actually tap into his retirement savings. Basically, funding would be needed to actually supplement our income and help us afford health care up until Social Security hit, most likely at age sixty-five or sixty-seven. With Mark's guidance, we bought a large universal variable life insurance policy with a monthly investment, nearly identical to what our mortgage cost was. The intention was to let the policy value build and grow so that Greg and I could take withdrawals from it as income to fund our lives from his retirement until, possibly, sixty-five. With that decision made and implemented, we felt set. And we flew back over to Rome in 2007.

Knowing that we had our finances squared away and a plan in place to save and earn more income moving forward, we wanted to maximize the opportunities living abroad held for our children. We wanted Connor, Katie, and Squish to cherish new cultures, travel, and enjoy the blessings of the world. This was something that two adult children from blue-collar families never thought they'd be able to do or afford with a family of five. We learned a lot as a family and Greg's work schedule actually pulled back a bit. To have Greg present in our lives for dinner every day let us focus on each other and build our own emotional wealth as a family. Our family's strength grew, and so did our bank account as we saved diligently over these years.

When we came home to the States in 2011, we had enough money for a downpayment on Greg's dream house, a wonderful home in the town of Nazareth, Pennsylvania, with not a tree or a leaf to pick up! The house was an hour and ten-minute commute from his work . He would wake at four in the morning, eat a bowl of oatmeal, shower, and be on the road to work by four-forty-five. Between the need to be in the office well after traditional work hours, and the long commute, he would come home nightly between eight and nine-thirty, long after the kids were tucked into bed.

In our minds, living a bit farther away from his job was worth it. We could afford a larger home by being farther from the city, and if he ever got transferred back to our hometown of Philadelphia, Nazareth would still be a manageable commute. I was thrilled that this meant wouldn't have to move the kids and they could start growing their American roots here in Nazareth. I was home...deep exhale.

My sense of peace was short-lived and those next two years were bumpy. Greg's work was challenging. His undiagnosed depression was like an elephant in the room. He get help from a psychologist and our family doctor. We realized as a couple that there needed to be a change; he was sinking.

The financial triage on my part began again. Questions like, "Can we afford to raise the kids if Greg steps away from work and I find a job working full time?" and "Am I advocating for Greg well enough with his doctors?" raced through my head day and night. During his days of clarity, we sat as a couple, and he would question me about money and savings, as I handled that aspect of our marriage. Together, we put a new plan in place. We made a financial decision to move back to the Philadelphia area so that Greg could take a step down at work to a less stressful job. We wanted Greg to be back at home, near his brothers and sisters where he'd always felt safe, secure, and supported. For the two years after we'd returned from Italy, Greg's relationship with the kids had become a kiss on their heads as they slept. One kiss each morning. One kiss each night. The kids and I wanted Greg to have dinner with us again, just like he had when we lived in Rome. We wanted to hug him, and for him to hug us, each morning he left for work, not just stolen kisses in the dark.

Greg switched positions in his agency and relocated to the Philadelphia area where he lived with his brother as I stayed behind to sell the Nazareth home and let the kids finish their school year. A second move and home purchase in less than eighteen-months put financial stress on us. We used all our savings to put a down payment on another home in the Philly area, in a neighborhood called Glenside. The Glenside home was the smallest home we had ever lived in together, but it was a wonderful, short commute to his downtown office. We had dinner as a family every night, the table was filled with laughter. Greg's welcomed sarcasm made the kids laugh so hard that they would have to excuse themselves from the table. We were back! We were also near both of our extended families, enjoying the support and love we had missed during our years away from the Philadelphia area.

Greg's mental state was better. He had found a good local psychologist to continue with the counseling he needed. He was in a good spot, and I truly believed the move and job change were the magic keys. Very soon after our move back to Philadelphia, our kids were enrolled in school and group sports . We spent every weekend that fall meeting new neighbors and arranging play dates with new school classmates. I declared to the kids that this was home. No more moves.

Two days after our first Halloween trick or treating in the new neighborhood, Greg took his own life.

SOON AFTER THE FIRST, NEVER ENDING FORTY-EIGHT-hours of hell, I realized my best friend, support, and confidant was truly gone. The magnitude of it all sunk in. Now, I had to make a multitude of decisions about my family's financial future on my own. It became abundantly clear the financial decisions and the sacrifices we had made to move back to Philadelphia were quickly catching up to me. Our savings and resources were gone because of the quick move. Greg's income had been lowered when he took a step down at work. And I was only working part time, making $17,500 a year as an aide in the kids' schools.

I needed help, specifically financial guidance, someone who could hold my hand and help me make financial decisions. I needed someone who could help me feel inspired and confident in my own ability to do so. Early on after Greg's loss, like eighty percent of women who switch financial professionals after the loss of a spouse, I did too. Mark, our financial advisor who had helped us feel squared away, had pivoted to working primarily with succession plans in family business. I knew I needed someone who could help me with my specific situation, so I looked for a financial advisor who had experience working with widows.

I found a new advisor through a referral from a friend who had been widowed years before. For the next few years, my advisor and I worked closely to put the pieces of my life back together, slowly, methodically, and with intention. We started off with an initial financial plan and took care of the decisions that had to be made in a timely manner.

After that, we revisited the plan as life, income, and educational goals for my kids changed. To be honest, it took me about eight years to feel like I had my groove back…to feel financially proud, secure, and inline. I didn't do any of it alone. I found the various professionals that I needed who walked me through my most difficult moments. By professionals, I mean my accountant, insurance agent, estate attorney, realtor, and therapist. These men and women, especially my new advisor, were my role models for what I do today in helping families get control of their finances.

Many families that I knew in the same or similar situations were not as lucky to have the right financial professional helping them, and their financial picture looked confusing, and sometimes grim. It broke my heart to see their continued suffering. The loss of their spouse was bad enough. This is where I got my inspiration to help other families in transition, like mine, with their financial clarity and future goals. By 2017, I flipped my career on its head and became a financial advisor for families in transition. My passion is to hold the hands of my widows and widowers as they navigate the first few years of widowhood with their heart, soul, and finances intact. My goal is to help guide them through the roadmap of decisions that have to be made after we lose a spouse or partner, identify their options, understand their financial strengths, and help them along the journey to this new life that they never expected to have.

IN THE PAGES TO FOLLOW, YOU WILL READ A LITTLE BIT more about the first few days after I lost Greg…and the first few weeks…and the first few months. You will read about how I slowly started taking control of my life and my financial future.

I wrote this book so that the journey and the learning curve can be a bit shorter for you. I need you to know that you have someone in your corner as you work through these pages. I hope you can feel my hugs.

MY STORY OF LOSS

THE NIGHT GREG DIED, I SAT IN MY GLENSIDE NEIGHBOR'S backyard next to her fire pit warming myself from the early November evening's chill. Halloween was two days prior, and the joyful giggles of the neighborhood kids were all gone from the darkened streets. I sat next to the burning embers, wrapped in an oversized blanket, insanely hoping that blanket would catch a spark and set me on fire so I could end my nightmare. Every now and then, my sister or my neighbor came into the backyard to check on me and give me an update, interrupting my train of thought.

The update would either be about my kids with reassurance that they were okay, or a gentle warning that a police officer was headed my way to ask some more questions. Although I knew the endless parade of officers were there to help, I breathed a deep sigh and stared back into the fire, dreading another interview with hope, once again, that the blanket I was wrapped in would catch fire quickly, putting me out of my misery. My sister, who had effectively swooped in and taken control of the chaos that ensued after I found Greg's body, easily recognized the flatness of my stare. She dragged my chair, with me in it, three feet back away from the flames.

As I stared into the flames, my thoughts tunneled through what had happened in the previous hour. I will never forget the pit in my stomach when I touched the doorknob to our master bedroom, and found it locked. I held my breath.

The panic and sweat that rolled down my back sent cold shivers through my bones. My three babies were in the house. I didn't want them to see what was behind the door. Our Irish Setter, Keaton, stood next to me as if he knew what awaited me and wasn't going to let me go in alone. I unlocked the door with a bobby pin...I stuck that lightly crimped pin, one like those I had worn in so many dance recitals as a child, through that little hole in the doorknob and I heard a pop. Without taking a new breath, I glanced left to see our made perfectly made king-sized bed, the one we used to borrow sheets from to collect the leaves in our New Jersey home.

I let go of my breath and exhaled as if to whisper to the soul of my lost husband, "No, Greg, no." As I naturally inhaled again, I could smell the blood. I could smell the urine. I could smell the hours of warm decomposition.

With the calmness and adrenaline of pure fear for my kids, I closed the door and locked it tight. I gathered a new breath in the fresh air of the hallway and walked pointedly to let the kids know that that their Daddy needed help. They needed to come outside with me, so I could get them a ride to my sister Sharlene's house. My goal was to get them away from the home before I called 911 so they wouldn't hear the sirens.

My neighbors who shared my front lawn were having some kids over to play in their backyard and enjoy campfire songs around their firepit. I walked up to my neighbor Linda, who stood by her back fence casually chatting with a friend, and asked her if her husband David could drive my kids to sister's house, five minutes away. Linda saw my stoic-pale face, nodded, and got her husband.

He quickly came from his house, car keys in hand, and asked me what was going on as his wife stood with her supportive hand on my shoulder.

"Greg shot himself," I said.

And with that Linda moved seamlessly into motion emptying the backyard of her little, unassuming guests. David swiftly helped me gather Connor, Katie, and James from my front steps, where they sat like the stone statues of Rome, and into his car.

David departed to deliver my kids to safety and moments later, Linda took the cell phone away from my ear after I dialed 911. Linda witnessed my "frozen tongue," a condition where fright makes you unable to talk in the midst of a terrifying situation. I couldn't tell the 911 dispatcher what happened. I was mute. Linda said the words instead.

I am not sure how I got there, but soon I sat in the loneliness of my neighbor's backyard. My sweet neighbors wrapped me in a blanket and sat me next to their bonfire, the one they had made earlier in the night for neighborhood guests to toast marshmallows and eat s'mores.

From their backyard, only six feet from my own, I felt and heard the panic of the activity from the street. The lights from the police car and emergency responders parked in front of my little home reflected off the house's white aluminum siding and again off the back darkness of the trees. I took deep breaths again and again. Long inhales, I told myself. *Fill your lungs...expand them...hold...focus on your breath and blow out.*

After my breath left my body, I took another deep sigh of air...and I started writing to-do lists on a napkin I had in my pocket, using a Sharpie I found on my neighbors' picnic table. My sister came to sit with me in their backyard. She took the Sharpie from my hand and began taking my dictations like a court stenographer. Then, my diligent sister started to put the plans into action.

She called Greg's best friends and let them know we wouldn't be making it to dinner that night at seven. She also made the tough calls. As she was on the phone, talking privately on the side of the house so I couldn't hear, I reclaimed my bold and sturdy borrowed Sharpie and continued taking control of my to-do list.

In those moments, Sharlene let me run my own course and never made me feel like I was powerless, although I was numb and, to the outside world, looked catatonic with a poised Sharpie suspended in midair. Sharlene kept reminding me to stay centered, to keep talking.

She was scared that I would go into shock and afraid of me getting distant, becoming too absorbed in my thoughts that were held in the flames of the bonfire. She was afraid I would shut her out.

From the darkness and shadows, I heard her say, "You don't have to be stoic here. I know you. Breathe for me."

That is all I heard in those minutes, and in the hours that followed as I sat there unable to be with my children because I was a suspect in Greg's loss until the police could confirm the cause of death. Little did my sister know, I had mastered breathing over the past few hours. I breathed through every moment because breathing gave me strength and made me feel stronger.

The smell of burning cherry wood in the fire will forever bring me back to that moment. But the air that filled my lungs, centered me. Bringing clarity. Bringing focus. Bringing a modicum of peace.

YEAR OF FIRSTS

BREATHE

IF YOU ARE READING THIS BOOK IN THE FIRST FEW DAYS after a loss, whether it be sudden, from a chronic illness, or perhaps the end of a beautiful, long life…your first action step is to breathe. When I first meet with a client, and they share with me their story, frustrations, challenges, and concerns, I often stop them early on in the conversation to make sure they take an opportunity to breathe and let the clarity and pause in. I also encourage my clients to make sure they set a time each day for quiet, for reflection, and to plan the next minute, the next hour. To this very day, I live life in twenty-four-hour periods. I have long-term, short-term, and immediate plans for about everything, so I feel I am in the controlled movement going forward, but I manage life in simple twenty-four-hour chunks. I realize what's manageable for the day and what isn't. I also realize where in my schedule I need to leave room for a pause and a deep breath before I take on some of the big hurdles the day can bring. If you are reading this in the first few days after a loss, there are big hurdles in front of you. But you can, and you *will* handle them. I have faith you can. You have to take a big, deep breath first.

THE FIRST 24 HOURS

I REMEMBER THE FIRST TWENTY-FOUR HOURS AFTER GREG'S death like a slow-motion black and white film from the 1950s and not a fun one that Elvis starred in. When I reflect, I can see myself moving through those initial hours, making every breath intentional, feeling like I was not promised another one. I walked into my sister's house to find my kids huddled together like refugees on her sofa in front of the blue, glowing light of the TV. It was about four in the morning, and they were wide-eyed. I didn't take a pause. I went to the floor, went eye-level, and told them that their dad had passed away. We held one another until my babies fell asleep next to me, all four of us huddled on my sister's sofa, the cushions and pillows damp with their never-ending silent sobbing.

We woke early the next morning and headed to my sister-in-law, Greg's oldest sister, Cairn's home. Greg had four brothers and sisters from a strong, faith-filled Irish Catholic family. Both their parents had passed already, and now so had their baby brother.

Upon meeting Cairn's eyes that morning, five hours after I shared the news with my kids, I realized what had happened was all very, very real. I moved from numbness into guilt. I felt like my family, my Greg, was the cause for so much sadness. I felt like I had to do something to fix it, to help lift the heaviness from their eyes. I didn't know what the next best thing was to do but I thought if I did something, anything, it would begin relief for the family. I could start to fix things. Looking back eight years later, I can tell you these were ridiculous thoughts... but at the moment, they were mine.

 Your first twenty-four hours may feel like a suspended reality as your brain tries to make sense of the nonsensical. I wish I could be there to hold your hand. Sometimes, being able to take even a small action can help you feel in control of the moment.

For that reason, below is a checklist of what to do in those first twenty-four hours after you have lost your partner. I hope this helps you take that small step forward.

FIRST 24-HOUR CHECKLIST

- Keep breathing.
- Find something of comfort to have with you at all times.
- Determine if your loved one made decisions on organ donation.
- Call your loved ones, close family, and possibly, clergy.
- Surround yourself with a trusted group.
- Eat and stay hydrated.
- Locate your estate documents.
- Alert your loved one's employer.
- Reach out to your employer and ask for bereavement leave.
- Contact the medical professional or medical examiner for eighteen (18) certified copies of the death certificate.
- Report the death to the Social Security office.
- Contact a funeral home and begin making plans.

You can also download this checklist via a link in the Resources section located at the end of this book.

PLANNING THE FUNERAL

EVEN THOUGH YOUR LOVED ONE PASSED LESS THAN twenty-four hours ago, it's not too early to begin planning the funeral. After Greg passed, I was numb. I couldn't plan the funeral by myself. My brothers and sisters-in-law stepped up to make burial and viewing/visitation plans. Greg passed late on a Saturday afternoon, and he was buried early the next Tuesday morning.

I had planned the timeline based on the fact that most schools and government offices were closed for voting that Tuesday, so I knew many could attend. Then my in-laws took action; they were saints. My sister-in-law Cairn's home became mission headquarters. My in-laws met with the funeral director, made decisions, created action lists, and then came back to me to approve all of their decisions before implementation. The kids and I literally climbed into the limo the morning of the funeral, and I was not really even sure where we were headed. Although I cannot speak from my personal experience of losing Greg, in my work with my clients, I have discovered that these are the top four considerations when planning the funeral:

- Decision #1: Burial, Entombment, or Cremation
- Decision #2: Timeline

- Decision #3: Obituary
- Decision #4: Payment

DECISION #1: BURIAL, ENTOMBMENT, OR CREMATION

Keep in mind any religious or cultural rituals. I was a Protestant living in the Catholic world of burial and did not know if Greg was able to be cremated or buried in the Catholic Cemetery since he took his life. We reached out to the funeral home for guidance and then verified with our parish priest. Other options considered were using entombment or above-ground burial in something like a crypt, buying a spot in a mausoleum wall to keep his ashes, or bringing his urn back to the home. In my heart, I knew Greg would want to be with his parents, and his family would visit and honor him there for years to come. Once we confirmed he could be cremated and buried at his family plot, where his parents were laid to rest, we moved forward with plans to bury Greg's ashes there.

DECISION #2. TIMELINE

We buried Greg's ashes within seventy-two hours of his passing. When we made plans for the funeral, we did not even know if it was possible to receive his ashes in seventy-two hours. First, the coroner's office had to release his body to our chosen funeral home. This was tentative because Greg's cause of death needed to be confirmed. If you remember, the night of his loss, the police detained me in my neighbor's backyard while they investigated his death. Although the police determined at the scene that this was most likely a suicide, the coroner had to make the final determination by investigating the angle of his bullet wound, crime scene photos, and other evidence. Once the body was released from the coroner to the undertaker, they would need at least 48 hours to have the body cremated. We almost had to reschedule the funeral, but on Monday morning, his body was released, and the crematory was able to accommodate our timeline.

Because of the tight timeline, we only had a public viewing or visitation right before the church service on the day of his burial. A viewing is when friends and family can pay respects to the family in a receiving line at the church or funeral home before the memorial service. In our area, there is usually a night visitation announced and then a visitation before the church service. I have some regret about only having one visitation as so many people could not attend or didn't even have time to hear about the loss. In hindsight, it might have been good for me to wait a bit to allow for family and friends to attend the services so that they could take part in the celebration of Greg's life and mourn his death. He was an amazing, giving person who touched the lives of many through work, faith, and community outreach . For many, there was no time for them to share their appreciation for him with me and the kids or to process their own grief by being a part of the funeral services . For the kids and I this was all we could handle so I stand by the decision.

If you have the luxury of time, I suggest you give the timeline some good thought. Ask questions like:

- Are there any religious protocols you need to follow?
- How many people might need time to travel from out of town?
- Mid-week or weekend services?
- How much time will be needed for transportation to the funeral service and burial site?
- Luncheon or gathering after services?
- Private interment?
- Memorial or celebration of life later?

DECISION #3 OBITUARY

First, understand what information should be contained in the obituary. Obituaries can be very factual and basic, or if desired, they can read like a mini eulogy. Here are some of the basics:

1. Full name (maiden) and any nicknames

2. Date of birth
3. Birthplace
4. Date of passing
5. Cause of passing (optional)
6. The town they lived in at the time of passing
7. List of surviving family (spouse, children, grandchildren, parents, siblings)
8. Careers/hobbies
9. Life milestones/accomplishments
10. Funeral arrangements, including address and date
11. Where to send flowers, or what can be done in lieu of flowers.

If you would like the obituary to be an opportunity to share the story of your loved one, this is appropriate, too.

- Add his/her favorite quote
- Ask friends and family what comes to mind first when they think of the person who died
- Share his/her favorite things in life
- Detail some of those quirky things that made everyone love your partner
- Write down a funny story that sums up your spouse's personality

Second, decide who will write the obituary. It certainly can be you, but it doesn't have to be. Maybe a brother, sister, or best friend would like to write the obituary for your review and approval. The process of writing an obituary for a loved one can often be cathartic. Make sure whoever writes the obituary has good knowledge of the extended family and life history of your spouse. Make sure the person is able to write an obituary that will be fair to all the people involved in the person's life. Let me share a story of when the person writing the obituary was not.

My beloved maternal grandmother, Babci, and her partner, Al, were together for forty years but never married because of their prior divorces, religious beliefs, and children. Babci and Al "lived in sin... happily" (a direct quote from my Babci). They adored one another. They loved and fought with great passion, and I was in awe of their relationship and ability to work in sync together. Theirs was one of the healthiest relationships of all that I knew.

Now, not everyone felt that way. Al had two adult children from a prior marriage. Over my twenty or so years of spending every Sunday afternoon and every holiday at my Babci's and Al's home, I might have bumped into Al's children two times. In the last three years of his life, Al needed a lot of care, which my Babci performed in their home, by his side. His kids didn't visit until the final days when he was unconscious in the hospital. When he passed, his body, his funeral arrangements, and his assets were quickly assumed by his son and daughter leaving my grandmother with no power and no say. Al had no healthcare directive in place, no will including instructions or power of attorney for Babci. Babci had no rights for her beloved since they were not legally married, and she was not aware that a common law marriage rule was no longer recognized in Pennsylvania.

When the obituary came out there was no mention of Babci or any of us, his grandbabies. Insulting a member of a prideful Polish family is one thing I don't propose. My sister went on a mission. In her pleasantly persistent way, she managed to have the obituary retracted and republished. She extracted a public apology from Al's son to my grandmother during the start of Al's funeral service. Again, make sure the person writing the obituary is being fair to all.

Third, decide where the obituary will be placed. Obituaries can often be submitted to local newspapers, religious missalettes, and/or online at the funeral home's website. The cost is usually between $200 for a simple listing and up to $800 for more detailed posting. If your funeral home director offers to coordinate this for you, I suggest taking them up on this one. Spend the money, as coordinating submissions can be tedious. If you are doing this on your own, feel free to ask someone else to head this for you so you can have the headspace free for other things. One of the most touching moments and most precious keepsakes of mine is the list of legacy comments left by friends, families, and coworkers to Greg's online obituary. I collected the comments from this online legacy obituary and had them bound and printed into a beautiful hardback journal for each of my kids. I plan to share these books with them at their college graduation, with hopes they are reminded to model their father in work ethic and faith as they move into their adulthood.

DECISION #4-PAYMENT

Funerals can be incredibly expensive if your loved one did not pre-pay for funeral services or put funds aside for the same. Greg and I had no extra cash for spending at the time of his loss. I actually put Greg's variable universal life insurance policy up against the funeral costs as collateral. I was at my most vulnerable point financially, not knowing how I was going to pay next month's mortgage, and my rescue net, those life insurance funds, were sitting in the hands of the funeral home so that their invoice could be paid before I had access to the money. Somehow the funeral home's needs felt like a priority over mine. My ability to house and feed my kids was sitting in the hands of the funeral home. Weeks later, when the life insurance came through, the funeral home took their cut and then I went to visit them to pick up the remainder. The funeral home had a representative on board at the reception area to pitch me his financial services while I had the check in my hand. Not nice... smarmy.

To avoid this, if you're in a similar situation, I highly endorse an overnight shipment of the check to your residence. Avoid situations where your grief and vulnerability can be exploited. As a financial professional, I will actually go with my clients to pick up the check if needed, to simply play blocker and coordinate a stealthy exit.

OPTIONS FOR PAYMENT

Prepaid Funeral or Regulated Trust. Check your loved one's documents to see if he or she prepaid for their funeral or if they have established a regulated trust and put money aside for the intended use of paying for the funeral. Diligently search for these documents to avoid paying from private funds or losing the benefit. During our estate planning process I often suggest my clients put funds aside in an interest-bearing account to cover the costs. Another consideration is a small life insurance or annuity policy, often referred to as a funeral policy, so that funds will be available during the time of loss.

Personal Loan. Check with your trusted bank or credit union. You may be able to get a secured or unsecured loan to help make the needed funds readily available. The plan will be to pay this loan back after the estate settles, life insurance comes through, or when the dust settles.

Rainy Day Savings. Let's call it your cash reserve or emergency fund. This is why you have the funds there. If you are unsure you have funds to make ends meet for the next three months of your budget, keep these readily available funds available to yourself and find another means to afford the funeral.

Government Benefits. Because Greg was a government worker, we had an honor guard come to Greg's funeral. I had no clue that was available until our family called the Department of Veteran Affairs. Checking with the Department of Veterans Affairs will help you understand your loved one's burial benefits, including eligibility for burial at a national cemetery.

Employer-sponsored Retirement Plans (401(k), 403(b), etc.). If you are still actively employed, you may be eligible to take a withdrawal from your retirement funds as a loan or direct penalty-free withdrawal. Contact your Human Resources Director or reference the Summary Plan Description (SPD), which you should have received when you enrolled. If you are a federal employee, there may be lump sum benefits available to you, so reach out.

MANAGING THE COSTS

Greg's funeral was expensive for our middle-class family; it totaled over $17,000. We moved quickly to make all of Greg's final arrangements, and I had others making the best decisions they could according to our tight timeline. As a result, we defaulted to prior experience instead of asking pointed questions about costs and considering all our options. When I audited the total cost of the funeral weeks later, I probably could have spent about $3,500 less. My words of wisdom here are to take your time. If you are feeling rushed, know that plans can be delayed. You can keep searching for a funeral director who can support you. You can continue to consider other end-of-life options. You can take more time to let it all sink in and catch your breath. I have compiled some guiding action steps as you move forward with affording the funeral.

First, ask for a price list. Funeral directors, under Federal Trade Commission requirements, *must* give you a price list when you first contact them for information either via call or in person. Once you make final selections, funeral directors *must* also give you a signed statement summarizing your selections. If they avoid giving you this statement, it might be wise to move on to a different funeral home.

Funeral directors who are licensed members of the National Funeral Directors Association (NFDA) or National Selected Morticians (NSM) must adhere to a higher code of ethics (like I do as a fiduciary). Use the power of the internet as your resource partner here. Check out the reviews and comments listed on the websites or Google rankings. Have your friends and family post on their neighborhood chat boards to see what kinds of experiences others have had and to ask for recommendations.

Second, resist the sales pitch. You will be offered a lot of options: burial versus cremation. Casket style? Inside liner? Do you need a vault? The vault is the large cement box that the casket gets lowered into that helps to prevent cave-ins. Vaults are not required at every cemetery, so call and ask. Discuss what is necessary and what is not with the funeral director. Take notes. Color code what is necessary and what is optional. Bring a trusted friend with you to be a second set of ears.

Third, act like a minimalist. It is okay to do the bare minimum right now. If you choose to have a cremation, use the funeral director to have those details taken care of and then stop. When you are ready, you can plan the rest of the details yourself and with your support people. Maybe your partner passed during the cold winter months, you can wait until spring to have a celebration of life and outdoor luncheon after you have a private internment.

Determine what tasks you need to handle personally and delegate everything else to extended family or trusted friends. Feel empowered by making the major decisions, like where the funeral luncheon may be and then ask for help to fill in the final details like reservations, menu, number of servers, etc. You don't need to be bogged down with these choices unless it is something that you want to handle.

Before Greg passed, his family always prepared their own church programs, wrote their own obituaries, and had close family members sing at the services. Because of a photo banner disaster at the entryway to Greg's church service, his family now handles their own photo collages and tribute pictures. As I mentioned, my in-laws took care of most of the funeral plans. My sister-in-law Jill asked me for five pictures to be given to the funeral home. Four were to be produced into two large photo banners for display on easels in the front church vestibule as visitors arrived. She asked for one of me and Greg and one of Greg with each of our babies, Connor, Katie, and James. The fifth would be used for the prayer cards and programs handed out during the visitation/viewing.

The funeral home produced all of these materials. Because of damages to our home that occurred with Greg's suicide, I had no access to the house as it was being repaired and, therefore, no access to the pictures we had at the house. I turned to the online album of pictures I had uploaded to Shutterfly over the years. The first four pictures were easy to find. The fifth picture came from my cell phone.

Greg and I had taken a three-day weekend trip to Las Vegas in August before he died. It was our first American trip without the kids.

During that trip, he actually agreed to go to the Wax Museum with me, which was out of character and much appreciated as I adore anything corny. He spotted a wax statue of Sophia Vergara, whom he adored as an actress. Greg was fluent in Spanish from his intensive training for federal law enforcement officers. Her accent made his heart melt. It took no time for him to snuggle in close to the statue, put his arm around her (the statue's) remarkably small waist, and yell over to me to take a picture with him and Sophia. The smile on his face was ear to ear. That was the smile I wanted to share with everyone to remember his zest for life and his full-bodied laugh. That was the picture I wanted to use for his mass cards, cropped to focus on his brilliant smile and laughing eyes.

When we walked into the church vestibule early that morning, an hour before doors opened to the public viewing, there stood two eight-foot-long vertical banners, looking like life-sized film reels. The first banner showed two adorable photos of Greg and our two boys. The other banner presented Greg and our daughter on the bottom frame and, above, a 2x4 feet photo of Greg and Sophia Vergara. My sister-in-law screamed, covered her mouth, and looked at me with eyes wide and tear-filled. I burst out in full-belly laughter and said, "Oh my God, this is perfect! Look, kids, your Daddy died happy. It looks like he was married to Sophia Vergara!" In that moment, the heaviness of his passing and suicide drifted away. I am forever thankful to Aunt Jill for that.

See the Resources section at the end of this book for a download-able resource.

ORGANIZING YOUR DOCUMENTS

I AM A FINANCIAL PLANNER. THE WORD "PLANNER" IS IN the title of my profession, so I love organized systems. After we lost Greg, we were out of the house for a week. My sister Sharlene was there leading the home repairs and remediation work that had to be done before the kids and I moved back in. Sharlene took a week's leave from her brand-new job to lead the crew. If I needed any documents during that first week, which I certainly did, Sharlene was my go-to. Because my documents were organized by file folders, alphabetically inside a file box, she was easily able to locate the necessary items. If you are reading this book prior to a spouse passing or if you are helping a loved one after a loss, here is how I have my filing system folders labeled. The files are in alphabetical order, with what I consider the most important for your immediate needs in bold.

- Automobile
- Banking
- Brokerage Investments
- Credit Cards
- Education

- **Essential Documents (copies of birth and marriage certificates, social security cards)**
- **Estate Documents**
- Health Insurance
- **Life Insurance**
- Mortgage
- Medical
- Pets
- Retirement Investments
- Taxes

That first week, I texted Sharlene each morning with a "What to Gather" list. Today, in my practice, I have created a personal financial website for all of my clients based on the "What to Gather" list so that my clients have all their important information in one place. The website includes a professional organizer tab so you can list all those important contact numbers, like pediatricians, estate attorneys, CPAs, pharmacies, etc. Picture it as a virtual filing system, like the physical file box that my sister went to, with all your information. Scans of taxes, birth certificates, insurance policies, income taxes, school and property taxes, marriage certificates, etc., all in one place. My clients use this system to help prepare and protect their loved ones in case of a loss. When you are ready, I encourage you to reach out and find out more about how this website works so you can have this resource available to your family, too.

WHAT TO GATHER

- Auto loans/leases
- Bank Documents
- Safe Deposit Box Key
- Birth Certificates
- Burial Contracts
- Business Partnership Agreements

- Citizenship papers
- Credit cards
- Death Certificates
- Deed to your home
- Deed to any other properties
- Divorce Decrees
- Employer retirement plan paperwork e.g., 401(k), 403(b), employer stock options
- Estate Documents
- Will
- Living Will
- Power of Attorney (POA)
- Trusts
- Insurance Policies
- Automotive
- Home
- Umbrella
- Disability
- Life (term and permanent)
- Health
- Long Term Care
- Annuities
- Investment/brokerage accounts e .g ., mutual funds, stocks, bonds
- Marriage Certificate
- Military Discharge paperwork
- Copies, contact: National Archives and Records Administration: https://www .archives .gov/
- Veterans eligible for burial benefits: www .va .gov
- Mortgage documents
- Organ Donor Form
- Prenuptial agreements
- Retirement Saving, e.g., Traditional IRA, ROTH IRA, Annuities
- Social Security Cards

- Tax returns (two years)
- Title to Cars, boats, etc.
- Utilities
- List of Bill Payers on file (start a calendar of due dates)
- List of Assets e.g. art, jewelry, personal property

See the Resources section, located at the end of this book, for a downloadable resource.

THE RULES THAT NO ONE
TOLD YOU

THE FIRST DAYS AND WEEKS AFTER YOUR PARTNER PASSES away are blurry. The world is spinning. It's an emotional time, and you might very well feel overwhelmed. There is a balance between appreciating the kindness of family and friends and knowing when to set boundaries for yourself. During that time, your community, your friends, your family, those in your religious organizations, and your neighbors will all be there offering help. And be forewarned, many of them will offer help with your finances. I call this "The brother-in-law rule." So many of the widows and widowers that I have helped over the years seem to have a "brother-in-law" who comes out of the woodwork after a loss and expresses themselves as being one of the savviest financial experts in the world. They offer to take the responsibility of financial decisions off the hands of the griever and to move things forward for them. It is easy to say "thank you" and slide your important financial information over to that brother-in-law, probably because you don't feel like dealing with it, which is reasonable since you recently had your life turned upside down. Please take a breath before sliding that box of information over.

Money is one of the most unsettling topics for many new to widowhood, and we are yearning for help, so the "brother-in-law" swoops in to save the day. I encourage you to know that I have faith in you. I am letting you borrow the belief that I have in you right now. That you can do this. You can and will be able to take control of your own finances. You simply have to let the immediate reactions to your loss calm down to open up the mental space needed to handle the money decisions in the coming weeks. You will do this well. You will take care of your finances in time and when needed. You will find a list of *trusted* professionals to help you. You will thank your "brother-in-law" for his wonderful offer, for his love, and for his goodwill for you. But you will let him know that YOU have this covered. People are interested and genuinely want to make sure you are okay. But your finances are personal and private.

As we have mentioned before, outside of the professionals needed, find one trusted person to be with you on this journey, whether that be a family member or a friend. This trusted person can help be your listening ear at times and share information with others so you do not have to repeat yourself or your story again and again. Use this person to be your "blocker." This is a very valuable person to have! For example, my youngest son, Squish, played football, and so did his cousin, Faith, who was the same age. In middle school, Faith geared up to play with her beautiful blonde ponytail hanging out of the back of her football helmet. She was the kicker.

Faith had grown up with Squish and all his friends, so they felt very protective of one another. Squish and the other boys knew very well that their job was to make sure that she did not get tackled...that the other team didn't touch a piece of her uniform, not a strand of her hair. These boys knew that all the moms on the bleachers and sidelines, myself included, expected them to protect her...or they would really hear it from us. Make sure your trusted resources act as your blocker, like Squish and the boys, so that those looking to take your precious time and energy don't make it to you. You are the kicker AND quarterback here, and your trusted friends and family are your offensive line.

On the day that we buried Greg, my mother really struggled. My mom is a loving woman, and she is highly emotional. She was consumed with worry that the kids and I were going to be "destitute," and she shared this thought with guests as they arrived. Her dramatic sighs would rise out of the quiet of the church, followed by sobs and her husband escorting her in and out of the church so she could collect herself. I was eternally thankful that we only had Greg's ashes there, not a full coffin, because she may have been tempted to throw herself on top of said coffin if here had been the opportunity.

My sister Sharlene, who loves to fix things and is always eager to help, was given one very specific job that day: to make sure our mom stayed away from me during the receiving line in the church. I said to Shar, "I love Mom, but she's going to be overly dramatic. And I do not want her to get people in the visitation line upset, or my kids who are standing up with me in the receiving line." And the exact quote might have included, God forgive me, "I don't care what you do. You can medicate the woman. Tranquilize her. Put her on one of those baby leashes, please keep her under wraps." Did I give you enough fore-shadowing? Now picture this: We are one hour into the receiving line. The church was packed. The line wound out the front of the church, down the Philadelphia city block, and wrapped around the corner. The funeral home ushers frantically set up speakers to go outside of the church so that the people who would not make it in could hear because the church was at capacity. The guest book was filled, not one page left. I am serious.

I hugged an attendee in line and lifted my eyes to see the sea of people down the main aisle waiting in the receiving line and the side aisles standing room only. I felt someone staring at me through my back, I felt it run down my neck. I turned over my shoulder to the pew behind me, reserved for me and the kids, and saw my mother sitting in a praying position and staring up at me with crazed eyes. I searched for my sister in the crowd and saw her in the back of the church talking to cousins. I made eye contact with my sister and with all the sarcasm I could muster, used my arms to make a motion to show my sister my mom's location, like I was a ground attendant landing a plane. I stopped grieving for that moment and shot my sister another persistent look.

My sister yelled, "Oh, shit...she got away," and came running over to the pew to retrieve my mother.

When Sharlene arrived in the pew, I stopped again from greeting guests and paused the flow of the entire receiving line to shriek at my sister, "Did she only take half a pill? Give her the full one." My mom was a handful that day and my sister did a wonderful job of playing blocker.

Your trusted person can also take notes as you sit with accountants, estate attorneys, and probate officials. Make sure that his/her schedule is flexible so they can attend meetings with you and be your human recorder/stenographer. But make sure that person has your utmost confidence and has your best interests at heart. Clients don't love this suggestion, but I even advocate that this person sign a non-disclosure document or privacy document that you can easily customize and create online. And I tell you this for a very important reason.

After my husband passed, I chose one of my sisters-in-law to be my confidant for my finances. She helped introduce me to my financial advisor. She went with me for every visit. She took notes. She's the one who had power of attorney over Greg and my finances when we lived in Italy. I will always be thankful for her help. But at the same time, I felt embarrassed that she knew my financial situation. I felt in the future that each financial decision I made for my kids, for my house, or even in future relationships was judged a bit because she knew my income streams, my net worth, and my ability to survive in retirement.

Now I tell you, she never said a word. Not a lecture. Not a peep. Nothing. She was wonderful about it and still is to this day. But, in the back of my mind, I always felt as if there was the old nun in Catholic school watching me in the schoolyard and waiting to tell the lay teachers in the faculty lounge all about what I did wrong at recess. For this reason, I suggest you use your financial professional as your trusted contact. I ask you to protect your privacy. I ask you to always be your own anchor. You have this. The tides might be strong. The waves might be big, and your boat might be rocking on the surface, but deep underneath that boat sits the anchor. It's attached to the ground, dug deep into the soot of the ocean floor. It is dug in. It's not going anywhere. The finances and the feeling of insecurity may be swirling right now, but you've got this.

Remember, only you know your values. Only you know the direction you want your life to take, and only you know what you can and cannot handle in each week, month, and minute. Be your own guide.

EAGER BEAVERS

I encourage you to let your friends, extended family, and community help when they reach out. If they are asking about your finances be direct and frank, and let them know you are keeping that information private and that you have a trusted advisor by your side. (And if one day you have a weak moment when you share a bit too much private info with someone you shouldn't, like the check-out clerk at the food store, forgive yourself.) If curious/helpful neighbors keep dropping in for updates on your life simply tell them you are taking it one day at a time . Thank them for their outreach and kindness, and then share with them some other they can be helpful . I am empowering you here with a quick list of easy tasks to take off your plate and will help you redirect those kind souls who want to help. I call it the Eager Beaver's Helpful List:

EAGER BEAVER'S HELPFUL LIST

- Food shopping
- Make copies
- Carpool for the kids to after-school sports
- Reschedule appointments
- Find a local teen to agree to take care of your lawn, leaves, or snow removal for the season
- Interview dog/pet sitters/babysitters

- Do a little research on the best therapists or healing teas to help you sleep
- Shop for the kids' school supplies
- Pick up dry cleaning

There are many organized services that provide everyday task relief for families. A simple reach out to community support from schools, churches, and community centers may very well reveal a wealth of resources. Many times, those around us really don't know how to help or don't want to step on your toes. Share this list or ask them to coordinate an outreach for services that can help you. Their hearts will be fulfilled because you are actually letting them help you, and you may feel a little relief in your daily life.

CONTROL OF YOUR FINANCES

Your next step is to find a financial professional to work with who is a perfect fit for you. You need to be comfortable working with this person because you will be sharing very intimate information. Sometimes, conversations about money can be emotional, but clarity and honesty are a must, so make sure that you, the advisor you select, have the "bedside manner" you need. She will know you well, understand how you make decisions, and work directly with not only you but your family members, too. I want your financial professional of choice to be competent and make you feel at ease reaching out.

THE FINANCIAL PROFESSIONAL SEARCH

After Greg passed, I needed a financial professional who wanted to learn about how I made money decisions and who would provide me with a close relationship of support so that I could breathe again. I needed to focus on my broken soul and be assured that there was a responsible and capable professional there to manage the timeline and flow of financial decisions, so I didn't have to spend my mind space doing it. I wanted an advisor who could lead my "trusted professional" team. One who had an established, proven network of accountants, estate attorneys, realtors, etc., and would work to coordinate my introductions and conversations with each. I didn't want to explain my situation again and again, nor did I want to interview seven different estate attorneys. Instead, I wanted my advisor to have already vetted these connections, so I knew I would be in good hands.

Once I decided to make a move to a new financial professional, I simply started asking around. I let my network of friends and family that I was looking for a new advisor and started receiving referrals and suggestions. My checklist for interviewing financial advisors was not extensive. I could do a lot of background searching prior, so I was asking very basic questions during my phone calls because what I really wanted out of my in-person meetings was to see if I felt comfortable and safe with this person. Did I have a good feeling in my gut?

I actually carried a tote bag around with all of my important documents inside with the dream of finding the right advisor, hiring her on the spot, and sliding my tote bag across the conference room table like it was a hot potato. The problem of organizing my financial life currently and in the future would then be hers, not mine. I clutched that tote bag stuffed full of binders, paperwork, and folders to each and every visit until I got a bruise on my shoulder from the weight of it.

In these early days after the loss of a spouse, your capacity and time are precious. For those starting the search for a financial professional, I endorse a three-step process. First, do a brief internet search of the advisor you have been referred to. A lot of questions can be answered off the provider's website. Second, have a brief phone conversation with the professional before you go lugging your tote bag in. You can learn a lot in a ten-minute conversation. Third, find a time to visit with the advisor for an in-person or virtual visit for about an hour or so for a deeper conversation.

After researching twelve financial professionals, I called and spoke to five, and I met with three advisors in person.

Advisor #1 lived in a gated home, which he used as an office also (not a gated community; his actual mansion had a gate around it). This intimidated me. Moving on.

Advisor #2 was a young, kindly gentleman who touted the firm's team approach and stated that I may have the opportunity to work with one of their "girl" advisors. Next.

Advisor #3 was the advisor for the widow of the man who played the bagpipes at my wedding, a mutual family friend who passed away in his forties, leaving four young children and his young wife. I had heard she was doing well and had been able to keep her suburban house and work part-time so she could raise her kids. She and her advisor had created a plan for her to gradually get back into the workforce as her kids grew. When I walked into the front door of Advisor #3's office, I felt like I was entering a sweet, cozy living room that smelled like freshly brewed coffee (the kind with hazelnuts in it). During my meeting with the advisor, his administrative assistant, whom I had set the visit with, came down the steps to say "hi" and let me know I had been in her thoughts and prayers since I'd first called. I literally dropped my tote bag to the floor when I stood up to hug her. This was the team for me.

Six years later, I myself had a career as a financial advisor and opened my own practice. I developed financial planning programs specific to widows and widowers based on what services I wish I had available to me right after Greg's loss. I want widows to feel comfortable sliding their tote bags full of financial documents over to me to act on and protect. This is why my practice focuses on families in transition, for this exact quality of service, work, and relationship.

In my practice, I strive to make my widow's or widower's first visit to the office as warm and inviting as possible. From our initial phone call together to our first in-person discovery session, I want my clients to feel safe, listened to, and taken care of. Each visit has a purpose. My widowed clients feel the progress of each talk, gaining control of their lives again with each step. As a financial advisor, I tell all my prospective clients that there are three topics that we will discuss no matter what.

1. **Financial planning.** The importance of and the seven step process.
2. **Protection planning.** The role of insurance, especially life insurance, in protecting you and your family.
3. **Estate documents.** Will, Health Care Directive, and Power of Attorney and why you should have them in place. (I am not a lawyer, but I know some very qualified estate attorneys whom I trust to work beautifully with my recently widowed clients).

By sharing these three topics with my clients, we set the groundwork for the fundamentals that will be the foundation for our conversations in the future. Our main goal in working together is to help you understand your power in controlling your financial future and how best to protect your family. That simple. A conversation about asset management, or how we invest funds for our clients, will come in due time. If a financial advisor truly knows you, your family, your values, and what needs you have in life, that is when he or she can help you make good decisions about your money.

A client of mine named Lenore almost wasn't my client. Her husband had passed after a long battle with cancer, during COVID at-home orders. Three months after his passing, she decided to find a financial advisor to help her navigate the life insurance, retirement savings, restricted stock units, and social security benefits (after quarantine lifted, I got to see her very own tote bag full of sensitive info. She wins, hers was cuter). She tried to meet with financial advisors over Zoom while she had a house full of extended family living with her during quarantine. There was little privacy to talk about her financials and lots of listening ears.

During our Zoom call, I let her know we didn't have to talk about numbers; our meeting was simply a time to get to know one another, to see if we were fit to work together, and to help point her in the right direction. Through my Zoom screen, I could see her hesitation melt away. Her shoulders dropped and relaxed, and she lost that "This is a business call" posture.

By the end of our call, her brother and sister-in-law had joined in the conversation. They wanted to know whom Lenore might be leaning on because they had been that support for so long. They wanted to know that Lenore was in good hands, and each shared their story. Lenore shared that she had fear over money being available for daily living, and expressed her concern about affording retirement if she continued working her preschool job. She reached out to me that next week to start financial planning together.

I soon found out that before our Zoom meeting, she had intentions of using another advisor, but after our virtual call, she realized that the relationship felt sterile and wasn't for her. To this day, I feel blessed that she is in my life. From her and those who love her, I have learned a lot of life lessons on love, motherhood, and the support of extended family.

THE FINANCIAL PLANNING PROCESS

Once you have met with your advisors, collected, and digested the information, make sure you feel good in your belly about the person or practice you have decided to move forward with. Make sure that they have the compassion needed to work with a widow. We are a special breed and need a lot more time upfront and lots of flexibility in the years to come as our plans evolve each year, especially in the first three.

What I want you to know about financial planning are the steps, the time it will take for your plan to evolve, and your role in the process. It is important to me that my widows/widowers know how the financial planning process evolves so that together, we can determine our timeline. You can't shove your tote bag across the table to your advisor and walk away, although as an early widow, I begged for it to work that way. This is not magic; it takes time and your participation. Some clients want their plan done ASAP (that was me as a widow), and others need to move a bit slower or have no need to rush, knowing that baby steps are okay. Knowing the next steps, what is expected of you, and what is expected of your financial professional is helpful in knowing that you are in control and moving forward.

As an advisor, I make sure the timeline is shared and agreed to so that the expectations are clear and realistic. When my clients need a little more hand-holding, that is okay; we have the timeline to help us stay on track. The timeline is made up of seven stages of financial planning. Here is a brief explanation of the seven steps I use in my practice:

1. Understand the widow as a person, including what aspects of life right now she feels most confident in, and what are her biggest frustrations, fears, concerns, and challenges.
2. Identify and select goals that my widow needs to address right of way, and which ones can be addressed later.
3. Analyze the widow's current options and financial alternatives for this first year of life after loss.
4. Develop financial planning recommendations to help my widow move forward with guided decisions during the next few weeks and months, as well as recommendations on how to achieve a financially secure future.
5. Present the recommendations to the widow in a clear, concise, and easily understood process. Help them create a manageable action plan.
6. Implement that action plan according to a timeline and tasks and work as a team to get the ball moving.
7. Monitor progress through communication, updates, and good old-fashioned hand-holding.

CASH FLOW

How am I going to pay my bills? How am I going to make the next thirty days? Sixty days? Ninety days? The next year? Literally, those were the questions that ran through my head hours after Greg passed. You would have thought that I would have been grief-stricken and unable to concentrate on anything but my shock or broken heart, so why, in those long hours sitting next to the fire pit in my neighbor's backyard, was I running the family budget and balance sheet through my mind? I was grief-stricken and broken-hearted, and the way my mind found equilibrium was to push the emotional loss aside and try to figure out the math. Math felt safe, I could understand the numbers and find solutions. I had no skill set for a broken heart and fractured family. Do I recommend performing the activity of doing family finances within hours of finding out your life partner is gone? No. Nope. Never. But I promise financial questions run through the minds of many, and through the minds of those who care about us. Our parents, brothers, sisters, and best friends will all feel better if they know for certain that your family will be able to survive financially.

When the snow settles in your shaken snow globe of life as a widow, the question of "How am I going to pay my bills?" may very well sneak into your head during quiet times. When the immediate impact of your loss slows down a bit, when the funeral has taken place, and you sit in the quiet of your kitchen deep into the night when you can't sleep, here is an activity to help you answer that very question. This exercise will help to identify your inflows and outflows of money on a monthly and yearly basis. Where does the money come from? How do you spend it? This will help with an understanding of all that makes you YOU and what your spend is on a monthly basis.

HOW TO USE:

1. Download the grid from the link found in the Resources section of this book.
2. Find a yellow and a blue highlighter, or crayon.
3. Get a pencil and start filling in the information that you know off the top of your head.
4. Put down the grid.
5. The next time you have quiet, uninterrupted space and access to your computer or filing cabinet, where you can pull your paper statements or access online banking and

credit card statements to gather information, pick the grid back up.

6. Compare your prior answers from Step 2, write in verified amounts, and highlight them using a yellow highlighter. The unhighlighted squares will remind you of what information you still need to confirm.

7. Identify any blanks, highlight them in blue, and put the grid down.

8. Call or email your accountant and let them know you need some help with the blanks.

9. Pick the grid back up and have another go at filling in the blanks with information that you researched or that came to the top of your mind. Bring this page with you to your next visit with your advisor so they can help you with the rest. (Pension, life insurance, and Social Security numbers may not be available at this time.)

In my current practice, we have financial tools that help clients aggregate their online accounts, categorize spending, and track purchase history. This information helps to produce an audit of the client's last year and guides us in setting spending goals for the future. When the information needed is all tidied up, the client and I can sit and review the information, results, and questions and get the clarity needed. This smooth process helps ease the emotions or anxiety that might be present during the initial stages of financial planning together and helps get us to a starting point for deeper planning much more quickly.

One of the tools that bring my clients their greatest comfort in feeling organized and more settled is having their own personal financial website. This is one of the first things I implemented when I opened my own practice because this resource was not available to me during my journey into widowhood and figuring out my finances.

This website helps clients by keeping track of their financial activity as they move from the Year of the Firsts. It often takes a year of learning and identifying the actual monthly cash flow and annual spending before our widows feel in control. The encouragement and use of this website in my practice are driven by my own desire as a sole parent to feel organized and transparent with all of my finances and personal and professional contacts. I wanted to make sure if something happened to me, the executor and guardian of my kids had a clear roadmap and place to start navigating from when she had to make decisions about the money and assets available to support them.

Many of my clients cling to their personal website daily for budgeting. Some clients check into their website once a month as part of their accountability to themselves to stay informed and responsible for their financial planning. My one client, Diane, has the website as an icon on her mobile phone. She shared that when she waits in the minivan to pick her daughter up from lacrosse practice, she clicks open her website and puts her transactions into categories so that she stays on top of recent purchases and doesn't forget what they were. This is especially true for her Amazon purchases, which can range from categories like gifts, home cleaning supplies, and clothing. It takes her two minutes while she is waiting anyway, and it helps her stay organized and in control of the budget. The first Sunday morning of each month, Diane pours a cup of coffee before the kiddos wake up, logs into her website, and checks her net worth, investment returns, and probability of success for her financial plan. You see, her financial plan is linked to her website and reports in real-time where she is according to our recommended scenario for her planning goals. If you think a website like this is what you need to start establishing more clarity around your money, I can help. Please reach out, and don't go it alone; send me an email at hello@donnajeankendrick.com.

NET WORTH

With a full understanding of cash flow, the next step is to figure out net worth. This is important to many after a loss because they want to know where they are financially at this exact moment in time. This is their new financial starting point. Sometimes, a client was not the partner in the relationship who handled the money, and sometimes, all the information is not readily available. Therefore, I urge those in widowhood not to do it alone, to have a financial professional working by their side. While I work with my widowers, I have an established process where I help my clients locate and identify their assets and liabilities. By working alongside my clients, we find the information needed to help them feel in control and able to move towards the next step in their planning process.

For many of my clients, determining their net worth is simply the exercise of taking a mental inventory of where they stand financially—what they own and what they owe. I have provided a very simple worksheet for you to do just that. Here are the instructions: Download the worksheet from the link found in the Resources section of this book.

Use estimates. Fill in what you know. Breathe. Absorb the information. Done.

Your net worth will tell you so many things. Like, what percentage of your assets are in tax-deferred or tax-free accounts? What assets do you have access to now, and which ones might you have to wait until age fifty-nine-and-a-half to use? Understanding your net worth will help identify which funds are liquid (ready to use), which ones are fixed (property), or intangible (goodwill in a business). Identifying your net worth is helpful in taking that big, deep breath at the starting line to this new life.

My client Lenore was speechless when we sat down to share her plan and review her net worth. Her late husband had made all the large financial decisions for the family, and she took care of the day-to-day bills. They had a lovely division of responsibility and clarity around money during their marriage.

During her husband's long battle with cancer, the focus of their conversation was not on finances but his health, and she shared that he would often tell her that when he passed, she would be okay financially, "Don't worry."

She took his word and did not worry. After he passed and Lenore and I began working together, we sorted and inventoried all of her accounts, employer benefits and stock options, life insurance proceeds, etc. When it was all aggregated, and we shared the net worth summary, she realized she was a millionaire with enough fixed income through pension benefits and social security to cover her day-to-day costs of living. I remember the tear rolling down her cheek, as she whispered, "He always kept his promises."

PROTECTION PLANNING

LIFE INSURANCE

THE PROCEEDS FROM LIFE INSURANCE HAVE ALLOWED ME to keep my house and educate my children in the eight years since Greg's passing. I wouldn't be here today, helping transform the lives of widows and widowers, without the blessing of life insurance and the freedom the funds created for me and my kids. When working with my clients, I help them own their power in controlling their financial future and how best to protect their families.

Life insurance will settle outside of the will/estate as it goes directly to the beneficiary listed. In other words, the insurance benefit should not have to go through probate for the beneficiary to have access to the money. The funds should come to the beneficiary tax-free. When many of us have a contract for life insurance, our intention is to have the funds cover our missing income for a number of years, pay off our mortgage, and/or provide educational savings for our kids. If, in the past, you and your late spouse had conversations about the intentions for this money, share those thoughts with your financial planner. This will help with planning conversations in the future. One of my clients told her husband that he better go on a "badass trip" with the insurance money should she pass. We took that into consideration as we established his short-term goals, and I am thrilled to share that he had a wonderful European vacation with his children.

The life insurance funds may come as a lump sum, or you may be offered settlement options, which should be reviewed in detail with your financial professional. For many of us, we have never had a lump sum of money this large. The temptations may be great to quickly pay off some debt, make needed home improvements, or help out those we love...but remember, there is a time and a place for all of this. Your financial professional can guide you on how to best manage these funds, ensuring they are used in a way that supports your long-term financial security. The decision might very well be to pay off the debt and put new windows into the home to help you save on energy costs or simply feel safer, but right after a loss, there are so many decisions to make and so many needs that feel immediate, that the desire to withdraw and spend is strong.

With my clients, I often will sit and speak to them from my widow's heart. It is so tempting to run to security by paying off or buying things that make us feel safe and in control. That is important, but certain decisions can really impact our ability to support ourselves for a long life. Let your financial professional or me help you identify those immediate needs and place the funds where they need to be, whether it be 529, a loan payoff, a rainy day fund, an annuity, or a brokerage account. Don't be tempted to band-aid your emotions by spending too quickly. There is time.

One of my clients, named Nancy, had no true experience managing money. Her husband took care of all the bills and managed big family purchases like vacations and cars. When he passed, she felt very in the dark about the family finances. We worked together to uncover the debt and contact the credit card companies. We processed her life insurance claim. We sat together at the county courthouse, waiting for our turn to sit with the probate examiner. We sat online and shared the conversation with social security together.

In the end, she had more income coming in through her own new employment combined with her social security benefits than she did prior to her husband's passing. If she kept saving until the full retirement age of sixty-seven, she could maintain her current lifestyle into the future. All good, until things took a sharp left turn. Nancy and her late husband had always rented, and she shared openly that she wanted to afford a house.

Thorough financial planning is crucial. We had a plan in place to build her credit to qualify for a mortgage, and down payment savings over the next three years. An acquaintance of hers heard she had life insurance funds, so he offered to sell her his townhouse for cash so she wouldn't have to qualify for a mortgage. We sat together and ran the numbers and identified that, when she lost her Social Security Widow's Benefit when her daughter turned sixteen, Nancy would barely have enough funds to cover the association fees, let alone utilities and upkeep. This was not the course I advocated for.

Fast-forward two years, and Nancy owns the house. She waived inspections and moved forward with the cash purchase. The home was mold-infested and needed significant repairs to both bathrooms. The life insurance proceeds are all gone. She works two jobs to be able to afford the loans for repairs and daily living. That is why I always encourage my clients to try and hold off on large or long-term decisions during the first year after a loss.

For many the first hurdle is locating the life insurance documents. Many times, we forget about our older policies from former employers, or we misplace old contracts. If your spouse's filing system was not clear, the processing of identifying if your partner had any life insurance can be a daunting one. If you and your wife had a financial professional or accounting relationship prior to your partner's passing, ask him or her for a summary of accounts. There are many special situations that may be covered by nontraditional types of life insurance, such as mortgage, travel, credit, and accidental death insurance. Many of these insurances are put in place during purchase or when you bought your home. Check your origination documents for the same . Here are a few other suggestions for ways to locate life insurance coverage:

- Check for group coverage at his/her employer. The human resource department or annual benefits guide can be a great place to start. You may also have added coverage for your spouse through your own employer's company benefits.
- Ask one of your spouse's closest family members or best friends if they ever mentioned having a policy.
- Check with bank or credit card statements to see if there is an automatic withdrawal for annual/quarterly/monthly premiums (or check the good old-fashioned checkbook for carbon copies).
- Check bank statements or call the local bank you frequented as a family to see if there is a safe deposit box on record.
- Reach out to your home and auto insurance provider/agent, often we bundle these services.

Once you have identified if there is a life insurance policy, the company must be notified of the passing. This often starts with a call to the carrier or agent. There are forms (including a W-9) to complete and death certificates to forward. Have your financial professional help you out with processing these claims and explaining the coverages to you. In summary, once a claim is made and the death certificate received, the life insurance should process fairly quickly and funds can arrive within weeks of the claim.

Let's talk about my client, Lenore, again. Her husband battled cancer for about four years. The summer before he died, his treatments were going well, and he felt strong enough to go back to work. About six months later, a tumor was identified on his brain, and he passed within ninety days. There was life insurance coverage through his private policies, all neatly stacked and wrapped with a thick blue rubber band in the couples' safe.

Lenore's husband had introduced her to the human rescurce manager at his work so she would have a contact there to help her take care of his work benefits after he was gone. Lenore felt she was in good shape and that she had access to and knew about all the accounts.

After her husband's passing, the funeral home asked whom was the contact at the Honor Guard to call and coordinate the military tribute at the burial. This prompted Lenore to dig out her old hand-written address book to contact her late husband's military buddies to let them know about his passing. In conversations with this group of friends, Lenore learned about her husband's employment with GE in his early years, post-military. She also learned that he boasted to these same friends how he had stock in the company. Lenore had never heard anything about it, so we went searching for the stock. Deep in the basement, in a big old Tupperware container that had been moved from shelf to shelf over the years, Lenore found the original stock certificates. Along with those, she found whole-life policies purchased years ago.

She came to my office with the documents, and we began researching. After nearly four full workdays, we found a way to move the GE stocks to electronic form and identified the new insurance company responsible for the value of the whole life policy. Imagine if Lenore had never thought to ask more questions to that group of old military friends. She would have missed out on about $130,000 in stock value. I kid you not.

HEALTH INSURANCE: YOUR OPTIONS AFTER LOSS

For many, their deceased spouse was the primary breadwinner whose loss of income is compounded by a loss of benefits. The most important of which is health insurance, if you are under sixty-five and not eligible for Medicare yet, there are some time-sensitive moves that you might have to make.

To protect us all from these fragile times, the government instituted the Consolidated Omnibus Budget Reconciliation Act of 1986, more commonly known as COBRA. COBRA is a federal law that requires most large employers (more than twenty employees) to allow you to continue coverage after a loss for up to thirty-six months. There are other options out there for health coverage, and you should explore them, but for the immediate need for coverage, COBRA is a great option because your current coverage remains the same, and there is no need to take a health assessment to prequalify.

Usually, the cost of COBRA is 102% of the normal cost of coverage (a little extra to cover administrative costs). As COBRA is an out-of-pocket expense, when the dust settles after our spouse passes, many of us start looking for a more affordable solution. The options out there can be dizzying. I often suggest to my clients that they search the Marketplace. The Patient Protection and Affordable Care Act (ACA) helped create the Marketplace for individuals to be able to find affordable healthcare options to meet their needs.

The Marketplace is basically where insurers and insureds meet, kind of like a dating app for insurance coverage suitable for your income and coverage needs. On the Marketplace, you will be able to find many resources and comparisons. The Marketplace may be either state or federally run and may also be the place where you can identify if you qualify for any federally subsidized or cost-sharing programs.

You may find out that you are eligible to apply for public insurance programs with Medicaid or CHIP (Children's Health Insurance Program). This all sounds splendid, but be forewarned, once you sign up for "more information," you will often be deluged with emails and phone calls for days, months, and years to come. Ask your financial professional if they work with a healthcare broker/agent. He or she might be the quickest, most efficient, and most private route to search out coverage options.

If you are approaching age sixty-five, you can apply for Medicare (there are several other exceptions that may apply). Medicare basics are Part A-Hospital Insurance, Part B-Medical Payments Coverage, Part C-Medicare Advantage, Part D-Prescriptions, and Medicap. Each part provides a different coverage benefit and should be understood before you begin the process. Medicare enrollment starts annually on October 15, and the window usually lasts until December 7. During that time period, there will be many webinars, seminars, and the like around the topic. Seek out a trusted source of information or a trusted agent/professional to help you. These decisions are important, and the options can feel overwhelming.

If you are under age sixty-five, make sure that your financial advisor adds a health care goal above and beyond your retirement goal so that you are planning and saving for each. Often, retirees think Medicare is going to cover their health costs from sixty-five on, but out-of-pocket costs and long-term care costs can derail a retirement plan if not taken into consideration and saved for. Having a goal for out-of-pocket healthcare costs in retirement as part of your financial plan is essential so you don't find yourself reducing your lifestyle in retirement by having to use those funds or perhaps running out of money entirely due to unexpected healthcare costs.

UNDERSTANDING YOUR CREDIT

KNOWING MY CREDIT SCORE WAS NOT TOP OF MIND IN THE days after Greg passed. But the question of, "Do I have enough credit limit left on my credit card to charge the funeral luncheon?" certainly was. The reality for those in widowhood is that our credit history, credit score, and availability of credit need to be understood as they can provide us with choices moving forward after the loss of a spouse.

Whether you have good credit, bad credit, credit in your name, credit in your late partner's name, credit in both of your names, and loans titled five ways from Sunday…you need to know where all your accounts stand. You will need to know this information much sooner than you expect after your spouse passes to truly understand your financial strength and to make decisions about how to manage debt, or how to position yourself well to afford a loan in the future. If you don't have credit, you are not alone, and there is help. Keep reading to find out how you can take control of understanding your credit.

My mom was a stay-at-home mom until I was in the fourth grade. That was the year my parents moved to a single home on the edges of Philadelphia for a "fresh start" to their relationship. Well, that "fresh start" stunk, and they divorced before I graduated grade school. When my mom applied for a credit card in her name, she was quickly told that she would not qualify for one as she had no credit history and no history of income.

My mom took care of all the finances in our family. She was quick with numbers, kept on top of her rainy-day fund, mortgages, and bills, and I remember her "envelope system" of budgeting. I have included her practical system as a little bonus at the back of the book. But, since she had no credit cards in her name, was listed only as an authorized user on my dad's cards, and had no income listed on taxes, she could not qualify for her own card. You can download my mom's "envelope system" worksheet from the link found in the Resources section of this book.

So, my mom went out and found a job selling cuts of meat over the phone. That made her miserable and she began networking through friends, neighbors, and church members until she found a job as a billing clerk and bookkeeper for an engine company. And may I give her props, she stayed at that job for the rest of her working life, saved for her own retirement, and thrived! Go, Mom! After a year, she was able to get a credit card in her name with a small limit that increased here and there with a good spending and payment history.

When my husband passed, all but one credit card company closed down our accounts without extending me credit on my own because I didn't have a long enough work history on file as we had moved home stateside a year or two prior. The one credit card company offered to keep an account for me, transferring the card number to my name only, and agreed to keep the credit limit (the amount I could spend up to) the same. This would allow the length of credit history to include the fourteen years we had been using the card. This length of credit history impacts your credit score, so it was amazing that the credit card company did that for me. They are my main credit card carrier to this day as I am appreciative and thankful for them. Loyalty and kindness still mean something.

Here is a little guidance on what to do first in the process of understanding your debts, liabilities, and available credit. The first step is to get a copy of your credit report. Your credit report is the starting point in understanding the strength of your credit, how much credit you have, and where we need to start a plan for improvement if an increase in your credit score is needed. The three major agencies to get your credit report from are TransUnion, Experian, and Equifax. You can get a free copy of your report, one from each, once a year. For more information, access www.annualcreditre port.com.

The first part of the report will validate your personal information. Review it for accuracy. The second part will list your account history. This is where you can review your limit (how much you can spend up to) on each account and what your balance (how much of that limit you have used) is on each account. Subtracting the balance from the limit will show you how much available credit there is.

Take an inventory of some of the older accounts that are present, that you may not have even known you had. You want to decide if closing that account or if keeping it open to show length of credit history is in your best interest. Most of the time, if it is a small account from a local retailer with no activity for years, it would be best to close it. The report will also show the number of missed payments and how long the account has been in place. Missed payments impact your credit score. Keep them current.

If you see any errors here it is important to report the errors to the credit bureaus because it can be a long process getting it corrected. Any court judgments are also listed here. Your credit score may be lower because it reflects this negative information or errors. Your score can remain lower until any appeals for correction are processed.

The third part of your report will show who requested a copy of your credit history in the last two years . For example, credit checks from the auto dealerships when you bought a car or applied for a loan will be listed . Too many credit checks done in those two years can bring down your credit score, so be cautious about how many times you apply for loans. Easy, quick credit is tempting in the first few months of widowhood, when income may be uncertain. Resist the urge to apply until careful consideration is taken. This is why I strongly recommend seeking professional financial advice as quickly as possible after the loss of a spouse. Our financial decisions in the early days can really have a long-term impact that we may never have expected. Remember, you are not alone in this journey.

Now that you have the report squared away, let's talk about your FICO score. FICO stands for the software used to gather your score: Fair Isaac Corporation. Many times our FICO score is not included on our credit report, so we must go to a third party to receive the score. Nowadays, many can get a free FICO number through banking or credit card relationships or from free or low-cost credit monitoring services (always be savvy about where you share your personal information online). The FICO score ranges from 300 to 850 points; the higher, the better. The average score for Americans is 716. Scores above 700 usually qualify for the best credit offerings, and scores 620 and below are considered credit risks for many issuers. Credit scores are negatively impacted by:

1. Too many inquiries over a two-year period
2. Inaccuracies in your credit report
3. History of late payments
4. Not enough credit history (not utilizing credit available to you can also hurt. Go figure.)

If you find yourself in a situation like my mom, where she did not have any credit history, there are a few things you can do:

1. When you call to report your loss to the credit card company on a card you held jointly, ask specifically if you can retain the credit limit on a card with your name. It worked for me!
2. Contact the bank where you hold your personal savings and checking to see if you can have an overdraft added to your account or perhaps a small personal loan linked to the account. Both can help protect your credit history should an overdraft situation occur with payment so you don't get hit with a late payment. A small personal loan can also help you start your credit history.

3. Ask for a secured credit card from the bank. This is basically where you put a few hundred dollars in an account, the secured credit card will be issued, and you can spend up to the amount you have in that account. It is kind of like backing up your own credit card! You have already supplied the money to the account, so you can have the luxury of using a credit card to pay instead of cash. You pay the card each month to replenish the funds in the account. This payment history will help to show a positive relationship in credit use.

4. Consider establishing your credit by applying for a gas card or retail card. Many times, retailers will authorize the payment because the loan amount is small. Please note, their interest rates are high. Be sure to pay off with each purchase.

5. Manage your credit card payments with automatic bill payment linked to your checking account or use your bank's online bill payer system. These automatic payment systems can help to make sure you don't miss any payments. If using the credit card payment system to withdraw from your personal checking, consider setting it to pay the minimum, so you know for certain no payments are missed. You can then go into the credit card system or your bill payer and pay the remaining balance.

6. Consider a loan with a cosigner. You are primarily responsible for the loan but can qualify for a higher amount with the strength of the cosigner's credit. Paying the monthly payments of this loan on time will build your credit history. Be sure the person you ask to be a cosigner is a person of trust and understands why you are asking the favor. My dad cosigned for my very first car, and that was one loan I certainly was *not* going to default on. Money with friends and family can be tricky; choose wisely who you ask to cosign.

Understanding your credit history and score is not just a step, but the cornerstone of your financial plan. With this knowledge, you can collaborate with your financial professional to leverage your good credit score for mortgages, loans, and refinancing, if needed. And if your credit score needs a boost, you and your financial professional can devise a strategy to elevate it.

SANITY AND SOCIAL SECURITY

THE PROCESS OF UNDERSTANDING YOUR SOCIAL SECURITY benefit at your federal retirement age can be daunting for many. Navigating the Social Security system after the loss of a spouse can be truly overwhelming, but it doesn't have to be, because you have this book, and a little knowledge and awareness can help it all move smoothly. Have patience, and take good notes along the way. Document who you talked to, when you talked to them, and what number you called. If they asked you to mail or drop off personal information, take a photo of it all prior or scan it.

If you visit in person, ask for a printed summary of your transactions that day. Have your financial professional help you navigate social security and your eligibility for benefits, your kids' eligibility, and your future ability to claim.

My personal journey with social security came about five weeks after Greg passed. I had an appointment to go in person to the Social Security office, and when I arrived, the line was out the front door and around the block. It was December in Philadelphia—freezing, grey, and depressing. Not much joy emanated from the others in line with me. Once I got to the line, I was given different instructions on how to receive benefits for my kids than what was previously explained to me on the phone. According to the agent who helped me that day, I needed to have three bank accounts established, one for each of my children, so that Social Security could directly deposit each child's benefits. Other widow friends of mine had their kids' benefits directly deposited into their own accounts. Go figure! I also did not qualify for a caretaker's benefit, but no one in the office could tell me why. Was it because I might have a pension coming in? Was it because we reached our maximum benefit? Today, as an advisor, I always try and give my clients a framework of what benefits to expect and the rationale behind them. If I am not on the call or at the visit with my client, my clients will have expectations set and a list of questions to ask should something sound different from what we originally discussed or shared.

After the loss of a spouse, Social Security may be one of your main sources of income. The size of the benefit will depend on your late spouse's earnings records on file. This is called your Primary Insurance Amount (PIA), and any benefits will be based on a percentage of the same. The first step is to contact your local Social Security office and set an appointment for a request. Depending on where you live, you will be assigned a specific office. The stay-at-home ordinance during COVID changed the Social Security application process a lot, which I am excited about. You may now be able to handle all of this from the comfort of your own home. During your interview, live or on the phone, the agent will determine which Social Security benefits you may be eligible for (if you are currently receiving a Social Security benefit and so was your spouse, they will give you an update on the amount you will receive).

Please note that the Social Security system may not seem perfect; have patience. Also, note that each agent will have his or her own strengths during your interview. Don't be afraid to ask questions, and have your financial professional at the visit or on the line with you. If the information or benefits offer you receive from the agent that day seems inaccurate (too high, too low, or even nonexistent—I have seen it all happen!), ask for a supervisory review. Here is a quick guide to help you be prepared for the visit.

Have ready:

- Social Security numbers for you, your spouse, and your dependent children
- Dates of birth for all immediate family members
- The death certificate for your spouse
- Your birth certificates
- The birth certificate of your spouse
- The birth certificates for any of your children under eighteen or still in secondary school
- Your marriage certificate: civil preferred over religious
- Any divorce papers from previous marriages
- Your bank account information for direct deposit
- Banking information for any of your children

There are over 350 different ways to receive Social Security benefits, including numerous combinations of survivor benefits, disability benefits, federal retirement age benefits, etc., which can certainly be overwhelming. Here is a list of the benefits you most likely will be seeking after the loss of a spouse:

Lump Sum Death Benefit. It is often called a Funeral Benefit—a one-time amount of about $255.

Surviving Spouse Benefit. If at federal retirement age (FRA), you may receive 100% of your late spouse's benefit. Now, if you also have a social security benefit, the funds received may be a combination of 50% yours and 50% your late spouse's. Feel reassured that the determination is made according to whichever is higher.

Caregiver's Benefit. If you are the parent of a dependent under the age of sixteen and make under the listed income limits, you can qualify for 75% of PIA.

Survivor's Dependent benefit. Children under eighteen or still in secondary school after 18 will qualify for 75% of PIA.

REDUCED BENEFIT CONSIDERATIONS

- **Retirement age.** This usually occurs if the beneficiary is younger than the normal retirement age when he/she elects to begin receiving the benefit (i.e., age sixty versus age sixty-seven, his or her federal retirement age).
- **Family Maximum.** Benefits can be reduced if many survivors seek benefits from the same PIA (remember, Social Security benefits are not infinite; they need to have limits so the system works). If the maximum benefit is reached, all survivors will get a pro-rata portion of the benefit. Please seek guidance from Social Security directly for this determination.
- **Survivors' Earnings.** If the survivors' earnings exceed certain limits, the benefit may be reduced. This can also happen when a spouse remarries.

In summary, the process of identifying your benefit and receiving the benefit may seem convoluted, don't panic. Have patience. Have faith that the right answer will work itself out. Like a splinter deep under the skin, in time, it comes to the surface, even if you can't reach it with a tweezer right of way. There is a system of checks and balances at Social Security that I have seen prevail with clients. You don't have to tackle Social Security alone; find a financial professional with experience navigating this with widows and use their experience to guide you.

DO YOU NEED AN
ESTATE ATTORNEY?

MY LATE HUSBAND GREG WAS A SOUND PERSON, EVEN-
keeled, with good judgment, fairness, and morals. For that reason,
even though he was the youngest of five, he was often selected as the
executor of his relative's estate and a guardian for his friends' kids. I
watched Greg settle his Aunt Kitty's estate (our daughter Katie carries
her name), and he was able to do it with fluency and ease with the
help of her estate attorney.

Aunt Kitty had some retirement funds that went to the designated
beneficiaries, all of her nieces and nephews and those recipients were
actually listed on the documents governing those retirement funds.
But for items like her GE stock and the house, those items didn't have
listed beneficiaries on any documents, so they settled according to the
beneficiaries listed in the will. It was Greg and the estate attorney's
job to make sure stocks got reissued in the appropriate names and
once the house was sold, the proceeds went to the cousins listed as
heirs.

There were considerations such as estate taxes, the cost of the
funeral, and the fee for the attorney that came out of the funds also a
bit of a math game at times. Greg had taken two weeks off of work to
start the process of settling Kitty's estate, which included sorting

through paper files in the basement to find actual stock certificates that were needed, and the two weeks flew by. He would often come home singing the praises of the estate attorney, who gave him updates, a timeline, and hints on what to tackle next, so Greg used his leave wisely.

On the opposite side, when Greg passed, I never had an estate attorney. The house, bank accounts, and cars were in both our names; I was listed on retirement and life insurance as a beneficiary, so outside of that, we didn't have any assets that needed to be retitled. Each case is different, but the main message here is to at least get guidance from an estate attorney if their services would be appropriate, and the earlier in the process, the better.

As shared above with Aunt Kitty's estate, many times, there are items like life insurance and retirement benefits that settle without the need for a will to be presented, outside of the will, meaning the funds go straight to listed beneficiaries. Most everything else will go to the heirs according to the directions listed in the will, and most likely, you will need the guidance of an estate attorney on that part.

Many times, you will hear someone say they are "settling an estate," which is basically recognizing the assets of the one who passed and fulfilling the liabilities, with the remainder going to the beneficiaries. An Executor is named in the will, and that is the person heading this process. If no will was in place, the estate is "intestate," meaning the state laws prevail in identifying heirs and nominating an administrator of the estate.

Perhaps the house was only titled in your late spouse's name, but the will indicates that you are the sole beneficiary of the home. Your estate attorney is the professional resource to help you navigate the process of having the home retitled. Not to say you cannot do this on your own, but in that first year after the loss of our spouses, the world is busy, and it is best to take off your plate what you can.

Settling an estate may not always be complicated, but it most likely will be time-consuming and a pain in the butt. There may be the issue of probate, which I used to think was a naughty word, but it is simply the process of the court identifying the terms of the will and implementing them. The will goes through probate when there is property to claim according to the directions of the will. Probate usually takes about nine months, and depending on the value of the estate, you may or may not have to go through the process.

To find a good estate attorney, the first place most people turn to is the attorney who produced their estate documents (will, healthcare directives, and powers of attorney). Perhaps that lawyer is no longer in practice or simply doesn't float your boat. Turn to your financial professional for a list of trusted referrals. Call and interview him/her. I always recommend meeting with at least three. Some firms are large, with a sea of attorneys to pick from and lots of supporting staff. Other firms may be sole proprietorships with a real mom-and-pop feel.

Work with someone that you connect with and have confidence in; that is truly the key. Many attorneys provide a free consultation to provide the opportunity to get to know one another, hear how the practice works, and see if the practice can meet your needs. Ask how the payment structure works: Hourly? Retainer? Payment after settlement? A percentage of the estate? Many times, there are no liquid funds available to pay upfront for an attorney; the funds are tied up in investments or property, so a percentage of the estate upon settlement is very common.

I highly encourage my friends in widowhood to retain an estate attorney should the need arise; in the end, the cost may be much lower than what a simple mistake might cost you, not to mention the value of your time. Remember that the executor is the fiduciary working for the best interest of the estate. If you are the executor, have your trusted contact accountant, or financial professional join you for all, if not most, of the meetings so you can pay attention and someone else can take notes on key pieces of information that you can refer to later if needed.

Since I mentioned having an accountant perhaps join you for a visit or interview with a potential estate attorney, it is only appropriate that I comment on this a bit. I am not a CPA or a tax specialist, so I am putting my widow hat on here. There are so many moving parts when it has to do with taxes in the year or two after your spouse's passing, that I highly encourage you to find a certified tax professional to help you at least in year one. This is crucial for ensuring that your taxes are handled correctly and you are not overpaying. You may still be able to file as married filing jointly (MFJ) for a year or two after your spouse's passing.

A word of wisdom: The emotional toll of literally checking the box "MFJ" can be big. I found myself mad at the world when I reviewed my taxes in 2013, the year we lost Greg. I saw that the MFJ box checked and felt like someone was sitting on my chest, their goal to push all the air out of my lungs. I was mad that all I wanted was to be married to Greg and raise our babies, but I wasn't any longer. He was gone. I felt like my identity had changed, and that stupid box on the 2013 tax return taunted me. To be honest, I felt the same way in 2014, but that time, I had poured a large goblet of red wine before reviewing the return.

If a new tax professional is willing, ask to have the prior two years of taxes audited for accuracy to make sure you are moving forward with a fresh, accurate start. If your spouse was the one handling the taxes in the past, have your tax professional walk you through the most recent return so you can become familiar with the terms and get an understanding of your family's finances. You may be able to capture capital gain exclusions jointly on real estate you sell and profit on in the first two to years after the passing. Your CPA or tax professional will help you understand what is and what is not taxable income in regard to life insurance, pension payments, social security, etc. I used an accountant who was a coworker of my late husband and handled our taxes in the years prior to his death.

PRACTICING SELF-CARE

WITH THE BLUR AND ACTIVITY IN THE FIRST YEAR AFTER we lose our partner, it is easy to get caught up in it all. I beg of you to be kind to yourself and have a plan in place should the overwhelm take over. Find a counselor, best friend, online support group, doctor, or psychiatrist and let him or her know that you are putting them on high alert. You may not need their support at that very minute, but they are the new National Guard for your mental health, and you reserve the right to call them into action when needed.

In the days, weeks, months, and years after a loss, you will be on the salt-n-pepper shaker ride of emotions. Some days, you will feel so strong, so driven, and so empowered to get your own clarity for the future. On these days, you will be getting things done, organizing life, and driving forward with a passion to take back control of your path.

The next day, you may wake up feeling paralyzed and unable to get out of your bed. You'll be unable to untie the tight ball you rolled yourself into. The dog will pee on the rug next to your nightstand because you couldn't, **wouldn't**, get out of bed, and you won't give two hoots about it. You might even consider peeing the bed yourself because you truly don't want to get up. And I say to you, you are not nuts. This is part of it all.

When my husband passed, I lost my best friend, partner, and father to our young children. It took me about three months to seek professional help for myself. I turned to my late husband's counselor and asked him for referrals. He vetted the referrals he sent to me, making sure they knew a bit of my background and story and were prepared to take me on...on a budget I could afford. Many of the counselors and mental health professionals covered by my health insurance were, let's say, not my first choice. I decided to pay out of pocket. For many of us, this may not be an option, so reach out to community resources for free group meetings or pro bono work from local professionals.

Within weeks of Greg's passing, I enrolled my three kids in Safe Harbor. This is a free service offered by a local hospital to kids who have lost a parent or caregiver. The kids met twice a month in groups, both age-specific and loss-specific, while their parents learned strategies of support in group meetings at the same time. To this day, I credit this program for the strength and understanding my kids carried in the first two years after their dad's loss. I also credit this program for modeling to me and the kids the importance of giving back to our community, volunteering, and compassion. To this day, we support the program financially and with our time as my kids volunteer as camp counselors, and my oldest runs one of the biweekly groups for kids suffering from loss of suicide.

Your community, friends, and neighbors may rally around you in the days and weeks after the loss. You will probably receive a level of strong support moving through the first year. Make sure to layer this support with your own system so that when the attention dies down a bit, because it will, you have a continued method of self-care.

Consider a daily routine that you can count on that may include yoga, meditation, exercise, or even an hour of reading your favorite book. I was a marathon runner before Greg passed and found that continuing to run on my own after his loss was the one moment of clarity and calm I had each day. I saw a sweatshirt the other day that said, "I don't run to win races or to get places. I run to escape this world. I run to quiet my mind. I run to feel strong, and I run to be free." Kudos to the genius who wrote that; how the heck did you get inside my head? Eight years after Greg's passing, I can honestly say that sweatshirt nailed the way I felt when I would tie my running shoes each afternoon after work and before the kids got off the bus. My sneaky forty minutes of mental repositioning. Find what works for you.

Outside of individual counseling, see if you can attend a once-a-month support group, go to dinner once a quarter with others in recent widowhood, or make it a point to have extended family over for Sunday dinner every now and then. Keep yourself connected. The blur of support will slow down partly because we modeled to the outside world that we are doing "just fine," which is bullshit. And because time carries on and the novelty wears off. You may push the support away because you don't want to be identified by the loss.

After the first year, I also followed my calling to become a Grief Recovery Specialist for the Grief Recovery Method®. Outside of my own once-a-week session with a psychologist, whom I lovingly refer to as my Skinny Buddha, I picked up a book on the Grief Recovery Method® (GRM), and it helped me align how I learned to deal with stress or setbacks earlier in life, and how that influenced the way I was dealing with Greg's loss. This method has helped me find clarity on how I make certain decisions, how and why I close and become "stoic" during times of crisis, and how I regard relationships in my now and future. I recommend Grief Recovery to anyone moving forward after the first year of a loss: https://www.griefrecoverymethod.com/.

The Grief Recovery specialists' programs are very affordable, too. This is not counseling or intended to replace any professional therapeutic relationship you may have in place. It is a journey of learning to help you identify how you process your grief through your life experiences and methods of coping in the past. Once identified, you can learn more about how you grieve and perhaps change course a bit if needed. The Grief Recovery Method is offered by specialists like me nationwide. During the COVID pandemic, the founding staff of GRM pivoted into training its specialists to lead the process online, both one-on-one and in groups. Consider it a journey of self-learning without the frills of buzzwords. The process explores the basics of who you are, what you did when you hit a time of loss or crisis, and the life experiences that influenced that action. You can do the method again and again in the years to come, learning more each time and respecting yourself more.

DAY 365

I USE THE TERM "YEAR OF FIRSTS" TO DESCRIBE THE FIRST
365 days we have to live through after the loss of our beloved.

- Your late wife's fifty-third birthday.
- Your fourteen wedding anniversary.
- Thanksgiving, when someone else takes your husband's
  chair by accident... not realizing it was his or simply because
  they felt awkward leaving it empty. (Greg passed a few
  weeks before Thanksgiving, and I filled my plate that
  Thursday, walked into a different room, and ate by myself,
  leaving my kids and table of twenty-two in-laws to get
  through this one on their own.)
- It's the first time you've hosted a birthday party for one of
  your kids or watched your son graduate high school.
- The life celebration on the one-year anniversary of the
  passing, or the day you dedicated the headstone.

As the Year of Firsts comes to an end, you can hold your breath
and wait for day 366 to come. I beg of you to look back and be proud
of yourself. You will have your support system for your soul in place,

filled with trusted family, friends, and community. You will have your mental health support system in place, filled with counselors, psychologists, faith-based confidants, group meetings, and psychiatrists if needed. You have your finances in place. You know your net worth, your flows of income, and your goals for the next few years, and you know you are on track to be successful in retirement.

I am proud of you. That took grit.

YEAR TWO

YOUR FIRST ANNUAL REVIEW

I LIKE TO CALL THE SECOND YEAR AFTER A LOSS, THE YEAR of transition. You made it through the year of the firsts, and now it is time to get your groove on a bit. You are no longer sitting and waiting for that new feeling lurking around the corner to jump out and get you. You have already walked the course and know where all the gremlins hide. You have surrounded yourself wisely with trusted friends, family, and professionals like your counselor, accountant, and financial planner. You have made a lot of the immediate decisions and put some decisions on hold. Year Two is when you can make the next set of decisions to help support your quality of life and your long-term and short-term goals. Set a time to sit with your financial professional and update your plan. Things may feel, or truly be, very different now. When you meet with your advisor, start from the top.

Share the flows of income like Social Security pension, annuity, life insurance, and earned income. Ladies and gentlemen, get your crayons and markers out on this one. The best way to communicate this is a good old fashioned flow chart or bubble chart!

Update on assets that you still own, might have sold, or obtained in the past year. Confirm how each of those assets is titled and the listed beneficiaries. This is the step I remember being bashful about. I had not removed Greg's name from any of the titles of the houses. Not such a bad thing, easily corrected, but I paid extra to have that part settled when I sold each house. The emotional baggage was huge. Picture this: me laying on my belly in front of the safe in my bedroom closet, looking for Greg's death certificate seven years later so I can send it over to my real estate lawyer to sell our investment property as I was exhausted with managing it.

Not only did I find the certificate I needed, but also our wedding license and our first-anniversary card. Those were bumps for me. And in true human curiosity, I took a read of the death certification one more time. Cause of death: gunshot. I was gutted and off my game for a good day or two. I was mad at the fact I had to manage that house for seven years without him, mad that my youngest was almost alive longer without him than with him, and mad that he killed himself. I promise you, I was most mad at myself. Mad that I hadn't taken care of this in year one or two when the wound of grief was open. Mad that I just ripped the scab off one more time. I hope you learn from my mistake and take your year two audit as an opportunity to button things up and free your future self from bumping into these things.

Obtain a list of accounts and summarize your net worth. There have probably been many new accounts, transfers, and rollovers of 401(k)s in the past year. First, make sure your financial professional summarizes and gives you a list of them all so you can inventory and keep track of them moving into the future. My clients have access to their personal financial websites, so they can download a list at any point.

Second, run your net worth again. This is your assets minus your liabilities. This number plays an important role in understanding your resources and strength of credit and can impact considerations like financial aid for college or how much umbrella insurance to have on hand (eee downloadable resource link in the Resources section of the book).

REVIEW YOUR LIST OF GOALS, ONE BY ONE

Cash Reserve. Maybe your cash reserve was set too high. After living for a year, you realize that month-to-month only costs you only about 75% of what you predicted or shared when determining your spending in the first year. You may have a streamlined life, so the costs of daily living have gone down. Many of us have not run the month-to-month budget or managed the daily bills before now, so after a year of controlling the numbers, tracking, and having real-time data to review, your actual monthly costs may be lower or higher than first predicted. Adjust your rainy-day fund accordingly—six months of what it costs you to be you!

Healthcare. Do you have coverage in place? If it is from your late spouse's former employer, how long will it last? Did you get a new employer and obtain coverage there? If you are on COBRA, can you research a better level and cost of coverage now?

Retirement. By this time, all your late spouse's accounts should have rolled over in your name. You and your financial professional should have shared a discussion about how much a long life and retirement are predicted to cost. Together with your advisor, you have set your goals for saving and know the return you need your investments to grow at. But remember, the first year has gone by, and maybe before, you were happy to keep busy and work until age seventy, but after the first year, you wave the flag of an early retirement goal and want to be out of the workplace at fifty-nine-and-a-half. It is so important to share these feelings of change with your financial professional so you can plan for the same. Your feelings toward retirement may sway four more times in the next fifteen years, and that is all good. You go with life.

Opportunities. Other goals like helping kids or grandkids with college, travel, retirement homes, and your concern over long-term care all play a role here. To me, these are the goals that need to be fully explored and discussed after year one. Why? Because when we are saddled with grief, sharing any hopeful future goals without our spouse in the dream seems wrong or disingenuous.

In year two and beyond, the reality of our loss has settled in, and many realize that it is our duty, our right, and our obligation to keep on living in the direction of happiness and forward movement as a tribute to our spouse who has left. They would have wanted to be there with us and their love is carried on inside of us. During the opportunity discussion with your advisor, flesh out all the goals that you might not have said out loud and see if they are possible. I wanted to help my kid afford college with just a little skin in the game regarding loans in their name. So, in year two, I sat with my advisor and "backed into" the amount I could contribute to their 529 without impacting my retirement funds.

AUDIT YOUR PROTECTION PLANNING

Home, auto, umbrella, and life insurance coverages. Provide them to your financial professional for review. If your advisor is not licensed in one of the lines of insurance, he or she may recommend that you get an independent review of the policies. Ask your professional for the names of an agent or two that they trust and who will not try to sell you hard. The agent should audit your policies to make sure they are in line and that your coverages are not excessive or that a needed coverage wasn't missed.

For example, we have a sump pump in our home. Our agent recommended we add a sump pump endorsement to our policy, so if our sump pump fails (which it did when the dog dropped a tennis ball into it) and our basement floods, we have an avenue of coverage available. Whether it be a sump pump endorsement or that you still have a spouse's car that you sold to your niece nine months ago listed on the policy, a policy review can be helpful to identify the things that need to change. You were busy last year, this is why your financial professional does semi and annual reviews. Remember, life was spinning ten months ago; things like this can easily be overlooked. That is why God gave us year two; like a rewrite of our eighth-grade history term paper, we get to make improvements.

Long-Term Care Insurance. This coverage allows for the protection of assets and payment for nursing home/at-home care should you need long-term care in the future. The coverages can be customized, and usually, clients pay premiums for amounts that can cover about three to five years of a stay in a nursing home. The average stay in long-term care in America is estimated at about two-point-eight years. Now remember, that takes into consideration people like my dad, who used his coverage for a big forty-five days before passing, and his mom, who was in a nursing facility with Alzheimer's for seven years. The coverage is there to pay a certain dollar amount per day while you are in care.

When researching policies, make sure you use a licensed and skilled agent who can explain the ins and outs. They should review the inflation coverage and different options for policies. Some work like a group life term policy, and some are a large cash deposit that can be guaranteed for a premium to be returned to your beneficiaries if you pass without using the coverage. Like models of cars, there are tons of different brands (carriers) and features.

You want to find the happy medium of balancing what fits your needs and what you can afford, predicting premiums into the future so you can consider if the premiums will be affordable when you are in retirement, perhaps living off a fixed income. The sweet spot for underwriting may be to start getting quoted for coverages in your late fifties if you are healthy and in good shape. Any earlier and you might be paying premiums for too long while your risk/need for coverage is low. Any later and your health condition for underwriting may change and the policy premium may cost you more or become prohibited. Fully discuss this with your financial professional.

Estate Documents: Once you have your will, healthcare directive, and power of attorney in place, I recommend reviewing the documents every three to five years or with major life changes. Perhaps you have not up-dated since the loss of your spouse. Year Two is the time! Especially if you have minor children. Make sure the guardianship makes sense.

Each year, on New Year's Day, I go to my personal financial website and print out a list of my accounts, punch holes in the left-hand side of the paper, and put it into my estate document binder. (I also print out a list of my professional and close contacts: Executor, Guardian for my kiddos, my CFP®, my CPA, pediatrician, etc.). This way, there is a roadmap for my executor to follow along with should I pass and a list of trusted professionals for the executor to contact to help them settle my estate lickety-split. Truly, after just going through year one yourself, I am sure you want to make life easier for your family and friends, God forbid something happens to you.

CAREER CHANGE

CONSIDERING A CAREER CHANGE OR NEW JOB OFFER IN THE years after the loss of a husband or wife can bring its own set of concerns. Whether you are making the change for quality of life, health insurance, self-fulfillment, or many other reasons, change can be unsettling. You have survived one of the biggest life changes many people ever face: the loss of a spouse.

In the first year after a loss, we tried to keep things as consistent as possible, attempting no major decisions or changes that didn't need to be made. The grief might have been about all we could handle. A career change can also rock our sense of security, so I urge you to move ahead cautiously, but yes, the time may have come to move forward. I am here to give you that little confidence push and also to help you take the scary parts out of making a career change.

If you are considering a major job or career change, I advocate that you go into the process with a clear, abundant sense of your own worth. I struggled with knowing my own worth, and many days, I still do. Greg's suicide left me feeling invaluable, and the messages the little gremlins in my brain would (and do) share with me sounded like this, "You weren't good enough for Greg to even want to stay alive;

what makes you think you can do this or anyone else would want to support your ideas."

Now, I know that is not true. I would hate for my kids to ever think that about themselves like that in relation to Greg's suicide. But the negative thoughts pour in. This message has run through my brain like an 8-track from the 1970s stuck on repeat. As I reinvented myself into a well-regarded financial planner serving those in widowhood, it was my gremlin's messages that would cloud the path. Mindset shifts, therapy, and the emotion freedom technique have helped me get out of my own way.

Trusted friends also helped. I remember this advice from a good friend as I considered giving my resignation to the school district two years after Greg's passing, "Staying in part-time work would be a waste of your talents. You have more to give." It was his words, reminding me of my calling, that I repeated and again in my head, until it became my mantra and carried me through the fog. I encourage you to find some trusted resources in your area and begin some mindset work and/or learn more about the emotional freedom technique. You can download a supportive guide to managing career changes from the Resources section of this book.

KNOW THE COMPANY

You are busy now that you are on your own. If a change of career is what you have decided upon in year two, then we want to make sure this process doesn't consume you. One thing to remember is not to do too much research and employer comparisons until you have the job offer. Yes, you must investigate the company and do your homework before the interview, but your time is limited, so don't overdo your research until the job offer becomes a reality. Spending too much time on company research might build up emotions or anxiety and leave you with a strain on your time (we all know the phrase "going down the rabbit hole").

Once they make you an offer, take a deep dive. Research the company using resources on the internet as well as good old-fashioned library research. LinkedIn can be a good place to start if you would like to get a feel for who else is on board at the company.

When a client reaches out to me to help them evaluate a job offer, I ask many questions even before I find out the starting salary, commission structure, and benefits. If I know he or she is looking for a new job, I usually share a list of questions/research to work on so we can start gathering the answers early and weed out positions that don't seem to match. If you are my client, I take a lot of pride in our relationship and your continued success. I know my clients well and like to think that I know my clients' drivers and motivators. Where do they feel comfort and when do they run to security? By knowing more about the company they may be working for, the environment, growth, and mission, we can more easily identify together if the position is in alignment with my client's needs and values. Without these preliminary questions answered, the salary has no meaning or relevance besides the math of dividing by twelve and seeing if the monthly bills are met.

EVALUATE THE JOB OFFER

Now that we have considered together if this company is a good fit for you, the next step is to evaluate the job offer, including salary, bonus structure, ability to promote, and benefits. Since I have a financial plan in place with my clients, we already have a clear vision of their income and benefit needs now and in the future, so it is easy enough to compare offerings. Often, a three-column Excel comparison is helpful. Label the columns Benefit, Current, and Future. List each benefit, like Health Insurance, in a unique row under the title "Benefit." Assess what the value is currently and what value it may have in the future.

For many of my clients, the benefit review is something we do each year during the client's open enrollment season. When starting with a new company, the benefits package can be a wonderful opportunity to provide insurance coverage, and I have seen some companies with benefit packages that make me drool. From nutritionists to legal services, ROTH 401(k), to HSA contributions...Hubba-Hubba! I get nerdy about reviewing these new employer benefits with clients as these benefits can really help us fulfill some goals of their financial plan, like getting additional life insurance coverage. A quick inventory list for guidance on what benefits to look for is available in the resource section.

The human resource representative for the company should help walk you through each benefit, but trust me, many times, it is simply a link to an enrollment webpage. Reach out to your financial advisor and have her review the enrollment page with you. You often have thirty to ninety days to select coverages. As mentioned above, your advisor can sit with you each year to review new offerings during open enrollment periods or Open Season if you are with the federal government. (The first advisor I worked for forbade me to call it Open Season. "Open Season is hunting season in northeast Pennsylvania." It may be, but it is also benefit selection time for those of us who are widows in the FERS system!) I update my client's plan with the new benefits information and then identify if we have to find additional coverage, or perhaps lower some coverages when they are duplicated with the new benefits. You deserve to always have a financial plan that remains updated and strong. Ask your financial advisor for this level of analysis and consideration.

NEGOTIATING THE JOB OFFER

I have no poker face. If I really want to work with a company and am excited about the job, every pore of my body shows it, and my toothy, eager smile and unmistakable giddiness defy any attempt to play it cool. Although I can't hide my physical reactions, one thing I am good at now is knowing my worth. I know what I have made in the past; through my financial plan, I know what I **need** to make in the future to support my babies, and I know the worth of all the years of education and experience I have behind me. I know the value I bring to the potential employers in front of me...and so do they...or we would not be at the table together.

Here are my words of wisdom: You never get another opportunity to set your base salary. Everything grows from this base. If you get a percentage increase next year during your annual review, it is a percentage of this base salary. Many times, increases are provided to income tiers at a company; find out which tier the salary offered is in and how far away you are from the next tier up. Remember, if you are salary and not hourly, you can often negotiate the number of hours worked on salary, with time and a half offered for anything over the stated salary cap. For example, my late husband had to work at least fifty hours a week. His take-home pay was based on forty hours plus ten hours of overtime. As Greg traveled often for work and was on the clock the entire trip, his hours quickly surpassed those fifty minimum hours. His pay above those hours was paid on a different scale or perhaps would be offset with days off.

Your next job offer, either with this company or with future employers, will consider the base salary you accept today, so take care to set up your future self by negotiating well now. What did you start at? What are you paid now? If you get recruited away in three years, that recruiter will certainly be asking about your current pay structure, wouldn't it be nice to say, "I got paid $X per year with a guaranteed money in incentives if I make quota, which I have done every year. I would need a base salary of $X or an improved package before continuing this conversation." I call that statement Wonder Widow Certified™.

Remember, by knowing and asking for your worth you are not only setting the bar for yourself, but for men and women who follow you. For your coworkers in the industry. Don't be afraid that if you put an offer on the table, the employers will rescind the job offer. Deep inside know your comfort with the company and if you are okay with the offer or not. I often sit with my clients before they respond to a job offer and I show them the possible opportunities to save more with the new position and the impact this career change can have on his or her financial plan. This way my clients know their income parameters before they present a counteroffer to a company.

The worst thing the new employer can say is, "No, this is our maximum offer."

You can politely respond, "Thank you. I appreciate you extending that. I look forward to working with you." Or, "I respect that, but I needed this position to work for me and my family. So even though this is a great opportunity, it might not be my opportunity."

OPTIONS WITH FORMAL RETIREMENT SAVINGS

Once you have said "Yes!" to a new employment position, have signed the paperwork, and have set a start date, you may have the question of what to do with that old 401(k) from your former employer. You have worked so hard to get here, to have your financial plan in place, and to now recreate your career. Don't let this be the time to have loose ends or what my dad would have called "straggling parts." Make sure you keep in control of your finances and know where your money is, where your accounts are, and how each one supports your financial plan.

Depending on the company's employer-sponsored retirement plan, you may have to wait two years after you leave the company to move/access your retirement money, like with a SIMPLE IRA. If you have a Safe Harbor 401(k), you may be able to move all vested funds immediately. Vested money is determined by the conditions of your former employer's retirement savings plan.

For example, the plan document might state that the employer will give you a 3% match for every 3% you contribute, and you are vested 100% immediately, meaning what you contribute and what your employer contributes is all yours from day one. Nice, eh? Or maybe you are 100% vested after three years of employment, this is called cliff vesting. Perhaps your employer's plan offered a graded vesting, meaning you are 20% vested each year and fully vested at year six, so if you switch employers at the end of year three, your employment savings will stand at 60% of the value your employer contributed. Remember, the money you contributed, is yours.

Usually, after thirty days of separation of service, you will have three options for what to do with your money invested in your former employer's retirement plan. First, you can leave the funds where they are. Second, you can roll the funds into your new employer's retirement plan, if they have one. Third, you can transfer your funds into an IRA.

Please note that as of January 2022, there has been additional guidance provided from the Department of Labor (DOL), for advisors like me regarding advice for our clients about their retirement funds. When we provide investment advice to you regarding your retirement plan account or individual retirement account, we are fiduciaries within the meaning of Title I of the Employee Retirement Income Security Act and/or the Internal Revenue Code, as applicable, which are laws governing retirement accounts. The way we make money creates some conflicts with your interests, so we operate under a special rule that requires us to act in your best interest and not put our interests ahead of yours.

In providing this recommendation, we agree to:

- Meet a professional standard of care when making investment recommendations (give prudent advice).
- Never put our financial interests ahead of yours when making recommendations (give loyal advice).
- Avoid misleading statements about conflicts of interest, fees, and investments.
- Follow policies and procedures designed to ensure that we give advice that is in your best interest.
- Charge no more than is reasonable for our services.
- Give you basic information about conflicts of interest.
- Deliver the Form CRS and Regulation Best Interest Disclosures as applicable prior to or at the time of the recommendation.

If you are happy with the investment offerings with the plan, the administrator, fees, and the portal, you can stay where you are and keep the funds in that plan. My main worry for many clients is that the funds will be forgotten about, especially if you are in an industry where you switch jobs or contracts often. I see many of my millennials with five or six different 401(k) or 403(b) accounts by age 35, so that means five or six different logins and five or six different investment portfolios. Another concern in this scenario is that with all the different portfolios, the investor may become oversaturated or not diversified enough.

I always remind my clients in widowhood to seek simplification. I support them consolidating accounts on their own or using an account aggregation system, like my clients' personal financial website. What I don't support is leaving hard-earned money forgotten about or my clients getting locked out of access to their funds because the plan providers have changed six times over a fifteen-year period. Words of a widow's wisdom: Don't lose track of your accounts and get professional guidance on how these accounts are invested, considering your plan goals, other investments, risk, and need for growth.

A great option is to rollover your former employer's retirement savings into your new employer's plan. This way, you can consolidate and keep your employer retirement savings rolling towards one investment strategy. Many employer sponsored retirement plans have downloadable documents for rollover into your current employer plan. Make sure you have your new plan all setup and have the sponsor information and account number handy. Most 401(K)s are hosted with a plan provider, a larger company that manages several plans for several companies, basically the company on the letterhead to your statement. These plan providers usually have trained customer service agents specializing in rollovers so they are very familiar with the process and can help you out. Have your financial advisor help you navigate this process, no need to do it alone! A word of caution: make sure you take a look at the fees charged and that you are satisfied with the investment offerings your new plan is providing because all your savings will be in one place. Plans usually offer about twenty different investment portfolios to choose from, so make sure you like them and have researched them well. Also know that you will be in charge of researching and selecting what percentage of your funds goes into each holding. There may be an option within the 401(k) that allows you to invest outside of the selected twenty or so funds and use many of the mutual funds and ETFs offered by the fund family supporting the brokerage window. This provides a great opportunity for diversification. If the last three sentences made your head spin, seek the advice of your financial professional. If you are like me and the words brokerage window get you giddy for opportunity, block off your Sunday, put on some comfy pants, and get researching options for investing your retirement funds! #WildWidowhood

Option three is to rollover the funds into an existing IRA or open a new one. Remember, tax-deferred funds go into a traditional IRA. If your 401(k) had a ROTH feature, those funds go into a ROTH IRA. One feature of a rollover into an IRA is that you can pick from many more investments outside of the constraints of a 401(k). A second feature is that you will also be able to have professional management of the funds if you would like to have your financial professional guide your investment choices according to your risk tolerance, age, and goals for the funds...basically according to your financial plan. Make sure you ask for a breakdown of fees for the investments themselves and the advisor's fees. The fee structures should be transparent. A final feature is that all of your accounts can be consolidated with one login and one statement, which more simplification and control over where your money is.

No matter where the funds stay, keep track of them. Use technology to aggregate accounts into your personal financial website. Print out the most recent statement and put it with your estate documents along with the website, username, and password. Keep control of where your money is and how it is working for you!

SELLING THE FAMILY HOME

As I shared in earlier chapters, my young family moved around a lot. Greg's government job gave us the feeling of being a military family, and we switched schools every two years. We had only lived in our Glenside home for a few months before we lost Greg. At that time, I promised my kids that we would not move from that school district. They could stay put, learn, establish themselves, and grow roots and friendships.

The house was in good shape, but there were a few improvements I wanted to make to help me feel safe in the home, like new windows instead of the glass windowpanes that randomly would pop out when the dog barked. New doors, front and back, also with no glass panes (I was traumatized by horror movies at a young age, you can use your imagination). I shared this wish list with my advisor very early on hoping some money could be put aside from income and long-term retirement to help me support these goals. I was relieved to find out that wasn't a problem at all.

At that time, I wasn't sleeping well, the loss of Greg still consumed my resting brain, and I became increasingly worried about the safety of my family in the home with fears that someone would try and break in. My routine was to put the kids to bed, drink a glass of wine, and put myself to bed in the same bedroom that Greg and I had shared. Lay there staring at the ceiling, thinking about Greg and that bedroom. I'd get up and relocate myself, hoping for sleep. I watched TV on the living room sofa, which was conveniently positioned four feet from the front door with a direct sightline to anyone who might break in through the back or side door. I fell asleep around 2 a.m., my hand clenching the fur on our Irish Setter, Keaton, who had climbed next to me on the sofa, after he was certain I was exhausted and asleep for the night.

I did get my new door and windows. I also made some major improvements to my kitchen and took down a wall so I could see my kids from every corner of the main floor of our 1,300-square-foot house. I felt in control. In the second year, my kids had found their voices through the counseling and experiences at Safe Harbor, and they felt free enough to share with me that living in the house made them sad. It had never felt like home, and it reminded them of their dad's suicide. They believed people slowed down in front of the house to tell the story of that fateful night as a source of entertainment. We were "that house."

My dear readers, guess how long it took me to put the sale sign out front: a hot second. The house sold quickly, and we moved to a fixer-upper in the same school district, on a quiet road with neighbors I knew. I lost about $40k on the home sale, plus settlement costs. The mental freedom of moving from that house was priceless and worth every dollar. After that move, I slept well for the first time in two years. The kids and Keaton did, too.

For me, the need to move from sleeping in the room where Greg took his life was liberating. For many of the other widows and widowers who I have spoken to, the home is where they have the fondest memories of their partner. It is where they remember being a young couple who ate pasta and canned beans in their early twenties because they were house-poor. It was where they raised their kids. It was where their best friends were, and the thought of moving had never crossed their minds. Many others have to move because when their spouse passed, there was not enough life insurance. This, coupled with the loss of income, can make the sale of a house a *have-to, not a want*-to. Each situation is different and all of us make decisions differently according to our priorities, wants, needs, and goals. I work through these decisions with many of my clients, using their financial plans as a starting point and modeling different scenarios of buy, sell, and stay. Besides considering the "what if" scenarios through their formal plans, often my clients and I start with the basics. We sit down with a piece of paper, fold it in half vertically, and write the words "Pros" at the top of the left side and "Cons" at the top of the right side. Then consider these thought probes below. A more expanded list of probes with explanations of each is located in the resource guide for download (see the Resources section of this book).

- Can I afford our current home?
- Am I physically able to maintain the property?
- Emotionally, do I want to stay?
- How is the real estate market right now? Will it sell easily?
- If I moved, where would I go?

I am not a realtor, lawyer, or mortgage broker, so ask your financial advisor for the names of some trusted professionals they may know; wise advice is always appropriate!

YEAR THREE

THE SECOND ANNUAL REVIEW

IN YEAR THREE, YOU MAY FEEL LIKE A TOTALLY DIFFERENT person. You may feel like the same person you have always been minus a best friend, but with the wisdom of living life to the fullest and giving back. Maybe you still feel stuck in the mud a bit, slowly moving your tires and inching forward. The emotions around widowhood are never-ending; you grow into them. Sometimes you have your groove on. Sometimes, the smell of perfume or cologne can stop you in your tracks. Remember, this is normal. Widowhood and grief don't end or go away, you simply grow with it.

UPDATING YOUR FINANCIAL PLAN

There have been many changes since you first entered this world of widowhood. Maybe you started dating again. Maybe you moved in with your adult kids to help with the grandbabies. Maybe you are starting a second career and are negotiating that job offer. Year Three is what I like to think of as the best example of what you can expect out of life moving forward. There are changes. There is clarity. There will be lots of people to share your goodness with. Most importantly, I like to think that Year Three is when many of us can start dreaming again.

If you have been working with a financial professional, the feeling of control of your money should be prominent in Year Three. You have a clear path for how to move forward into the future financially. When I sit with my clients in their second year of widowhood for their annual review, right when they are entering year three, I feel excited for them. Year Three is when we pull back open their financial plan and start expanding on goals. It is time to give my clients in widowhood permission to start dreaming again.

Maybe we add a travel goal, often an exciting one, maybe to a tropical destination for a family beach vacation or a big city for a large family reunion trip. In Year Three, we also discuss updating retirement spending goals so that the amount might be increased. A lot has probably happened in three years, such as additional income from a job change or the sale of a property. As advisors working with clients in widowhood, we are usually conservative on the initial amount we predict our clients can spend annually during their retirement years. Many times, there is a feeling of scarcity for our clients in the first year of a loss, and looking too far into the future seems unwarranted.

We have lost the one we love, the one we were planning on spending that future with. Now that some time has gone by, as advisors, we might be able to give more guidance on living in retirement according to lifestyle versus basic needs. Our clients might be able to imagine that future now, where before it felt painful. Does retirement mean launching that second or third career? Teaching and guiding young learners into your industry? Does retirement mean ditching the house, buying an RV, and traveling from state to state? Do you not even want to retire at all? They are going to have to push you out the door of your office on your ninety-ninth birthday. Updating our goals in year three can be full of excitement and dreams. I love hearing about them!

Year Three is when we take a deep dive into the long-term stuff. If you own your own business or have kept a family business going after the loss of your spouse, what does that succession plan look like?

Who could lead this business with your work ethic? Is the plan to keep the business in the family and provide a legacy for your kids or to find a third party so that the value of the business can help support your other goals?

I love what I do, but I am not sure any of my kids will share my passion for financial planning and helping families in transition. They may or may not be the succession plan for Sephton Financial. I want to keep working well into my seventies but free myself up a bit so that I can establish a Safe Harbor/Dougy Center type of program in upstate Pennsylvania, where I know the available resources to families in transition are low. I also know that in a few years, I want to speak more to those in widowhood to let them know to breathe through the process and to give them permission to look for rainbows and have a laugh along the way. So, how do I position my business and career to do that? Year Three is when many of us start to think more towards the future, not immediate survival like in the first year after our loss.

UPDATING YOUR ESTATE DOCUMENTS

At the beginning of Year Three, pull out those estate documents again. Read them over and update them where needed. Maybe the executor you chose moved out of the state, and you would hate for them to have to manage things from afar. Time to nominate a new one. My clients each have a personal financial website where there is a section to list contact information that might be needed in an emergency as well as a vault for online secure storage for pdf's of personal documents. I offered this because I truly wanted my widowed and divorced clients to have everything in one place. I wanted them to feel organized. I wanted them to know that they could offer their executor one place to find all their information, nice and tidy. I guide my clients through using the resource effectively.

Should you not have a system like your personal financial website, here are some other thoughts and considerations:

Make sure your estate documents have your list of personal and

professional contacts all listed. After becoming widowed, I became very private after the first year. Instead of confiding in close friends and family, I used lots of professionals to help me along the way, accountants, financial advisors, estate attorneys, etc. These professionals and their contact information are each listed in case my executor needs clarifying documents. My primary doctor and specialists are all listed, too, as well as those who care for my kids. From baseball coaches to the pediatricians. If I pass, I don't need my executor scrolling through the contacts in my phone to find Katie's Invisalign orthodontist; it is all listed here.

Attach a summary of accounts and net worth that you printed from your financial plan. This information can be used like a roadmap for your executor should you pass. They will know where each account is located and the general amount of the estate. These numbers are important should you or I pass as a sole parent. It is the executor and guardians who will be making decisions for our kids, and they will want to know the finances sooner rather than later so they can start making decisions.

List your online accounts and updated passwords. If you use an electronic password app, do you have the password to your password keeper listed? I personally get annoyed every time I have to update my password, so I use True Key to update my User ID and password automatically. My login credentials are taped to the front cover of my estate documents. Other online password aggregators are LastPass and Nordpass.

Share the details of what you would like done should you pass. I run a wonderful in-home wine party with friends and fellow widows called "Plan Your Own Fun Funeral." As a result of the get-together, you have a folder with completed instructions for the fun party that is to be had in your memory. When I pass, I've left instructions to have a celebration of life party involving a kielbasa truck and mini pierogi appetizers. Yes, I want to be cremated. No, I don't want to be sitting on a shelf in my kid's closet, along with the ashes of our dog. I would rather be mulch. No disrespect intended, just a little freedom from the heaviness of the event. One of the attendees to my last Fun Funeral party did a ton of research on natural burial, including topics like shrouding and what states allow it. Fascinating!

Once your estate documents are updated, ensure they go straight back into your safe or fireproof box. Call your executor and make sure they know where it is, where the key is, or what the combination is.

COMMUNITY GIVING

In Year Three, you may be looking for opportunities to help others new to widowhood. There are many ways to support grieving families. You can support those in your community through prayer, service, or even charitable giving. I received so much support from my community after we lost Greg, and I will always be appreciative. Many of us feel motivated to give back with our time after receiving such selfless service from others. Some of us may still feel too awkward or emotional being out in public with our message, so dropping a card in the mail, writing a check, or keeping a prayer list might be what we can do.

I have seen widows and widowers become advocates for a cause that has impacted them. It is that energy and calling as a speaker and advocate that becomes part of their identity. The need to make this earth better is deep inside each one of us experiencing widowhood. For some, it comes right away. For some, it takes years because the heaviness of grief remains. Simply remember it is in there; the loss of our spouse was not in vain, and you and I are the catalysts for giving back to the communities that need our love. We can create meaning out of the loss.

At the end of Year Two, I decided to start giving back to the community that helped me so much after the loss of Greg. I continue to be impressed and almost speechless when thinking about the unconditional kindness of my neighbors who rallied around me. The families on my U-shaped street and the surrounding block would literally drive past my house, even if out of their way, to slow down and check in to see if I needed anything. I would often have my front door wide open, with the glass storm door presenting itself to the neighborhood. Those neighbors would see the front door open, pull over, and honk. My Irish Setter would go nuts barking, so I would always go to the door and see what was going on.

I can't tell you how many times my sweet neighbors stopped by to offer to grab me milk and eggs, or their four-year-old would jump out with a tray of cookies for my kids, and once my neighbor dangled a bottle of wine out from the passenger side window for me to go out and collect. In addition to impromptu check-ins, the moms on the block would hear about the gossip spread on the bus from other children about Greg's suicide, and they would spring into action, reaching out to school counselors and teachers to help educate the kids about this concept and the kindness needed. Many times, the actions were revealed to me months or years later, and the ladies were seamless. Sometimes, I would catch wind of the gossip and see my advocates sitting on the front lawn of the parents of the offender, sharing a wine and talking it through. This neighborhood embodied kindness, support, and doing the right things.

I share the stories of my neighborhood because they modeled for me how to take care of our community, and they drove me into action. I led many meal trains in Year Three helping to provide meals to families in transition www.mealtrain.com. I made sure there was a bottle of wine or six-pack of beer and pizza dropped off on Fridays even after the meal train ended. I began giving back to the community in small ways that I could easily manage and didn't take too much time so I could keep being the mom I needed to be.

In the years to come, these givebacks to the community snowballed, in a good way. My support of Safe Harbor turned into organizing running groups for fundraising- ing. In 2015, we signed up so many runners for a half marathon in Philly that our team had their own meet-up spot with our very own Porta Potty. I now give about 10% of my take-home pay to Safe Harbor each year in Greg's memory. Along with the staff at Safe Harbor, I work on obtaining grants from my industry to support their mission and secured $20k in 2021 from Invest in Others www.investinothers.org/abington-health-foundation-grants-for-good-winner/. Decide on what moves you want to make and how you can make lemons out of lemonade, and go for it in Year Three. The blessings are amazing.

For some in widowhood, the passing of a spouse provided an opportunity for wealth that they were not aware of. It could be that his spouse took care of all the investment and the widower had no clue of their substantial net worth, or there were life insurance policies that paid out, and the funds were above and beyond the family's current or proposed future lifestyle. When that happens, many of my clients look towards charitable giving. I have also found that through the process of our loved one passing, our families have been touched by the goodness of others, many times through nonprofit services. My one client named Deborah lost her husband to brain cancer. When he was diagnosed, her family had temporarily moved states for treatment. There was a nonprofit full of good-hearted volunteers and two paid employees ready and waiting to help the family find temporary housing, provide food, and transport them to and from the treatment center so the family wouldn't have to pay thirty dollars a day in parking at the facility. When her husband passed, there was a $15,000 whole-life policy she had forgotten about. After we shared her plan and were pretty certain she and the kids would be successful in affording their future, she gifted those funds to the facility. I will always remember her tears the day we shared her plan and when she realized she could make such a substantial donation. If your finances don't allow for a monetary donation, consider volunteering your time or support via social media reposting. Do what makes your heart grow!

FORGIVENESS

I WALKED INTO YEAR THREE WITH A LOT OF FRUSTRATIONS. From my relationship with my and Greg's extended family to dating, to my parenting skills, to my studies for my new career...I felt like I was simply spinning my wheels and going nowhere. I wanted and needed all those things to feel settled and consistent, but none were. Why? Because life is everchanging and these relationships were not perfect before Greg passed, so they certainly were not going to be after he died.

It took me time to forgive myself for not being what I felt was successful in certain areas of my life. It took me time to forgive myself for cursing God for handing my kids a raw deal. I had to forgive others who had tried to help over the past three years but maybe stepped on my toes a bit. I had to forgive Greg for leaving us.

Once you add a little bit of forgiveness to Year Three, you may feel freer to breathe out some old stale air and breathe in some opportunities. In Year Three, really think about who you want to surround yourself with. I had a few clients who, in the third year after their spouse passed, simply moved away. They needed a fresh start. They dropped their Facebook accounts and started again somewhere new. I have also had clients who wanted to simply dig in deep with all the family, friends, and community around them and enjoy the ride. There are many choices that come to you in Year Three, and with it is a choice to forgive.

A LOVE LETTER FOR YOU

AFTER WE COMB THROUGH AND UPDATE OUR LONG-TERM goals in Year Three, I propose that my clients sit with me and write a Love Letter to their family. Sound corny? Maybe it is. This Love Letter is an opportunity to sit down and really digest your evolving plan with a focus on dreams for the future. Year One was a blur. In Year Two, we got our groove on. In Year Three, we allowed ourselves to think about the future a little more, without guilt, and with the hope of being happy again. Maybe even with thoughts of moving forward in a new relationship or making a move that we never even considered before. Things are different now. Things are new. Allow yourself to dream.

The Love Letter is a guided process, where my clients and I sit down and start a conversation. During this talk together, we cover topics ranging from traditions you would love to see start or continue in the next few years to what you would like to see done with your family home should you pass. I have even had a client share that he did not want any grandkids named after him; he thought his name was obnoxious, and his Love Letter message was to his adult children not to honor him with a "junior."

I love sitting with my clients to write their Love Letters because it is an opportunity to say their desires and intentions out loud, to make them real, to make their dreams feel less like "blue sky" and more like a reality. If I didn't encourage my clients to sit down with me and write this out, it might never happen. We have the right to our Year Three dreams, dreams for the future didn't go away with the loss of our spouse.

The best part is after we are done, my client and I can sit with their loved ones and share the parts of her Love Letter that she thinks will help give clarity on her mission and drive in life. Perhaps you'll share your Love Letter with your adult children, or with the siblings who have been by your side, or maybe with the people who have had you constantly on their prayer list.

I often sit alongside my client and lead the conversation around her Love Letter with those she has chosen to share it with. By request, I sometimes meet individually with my client's cherished family for a one-on-one conversation and review of the Love Letter. I find that it provides the family with the reassurance that my client is sane, hopeful, and in control. With the Love Letter, the client can share with others important information about her, about her relationship with money, what makes her heartbeat, and how she wants to lead life now. This clarity is a gift to my client's loved ones.

A MESSAGE FROM ME TO YOU

THROUGH THE LAST 100+ PAGES YOU HAVE BEEN PROVIDED a resource to help guide you through the first three years of widow-hood. The first two-thirds of the book was very heavy in navigating year one, and rightfully so; it is a lot. I hope the stories along the way helped you feel connected and human and perhaps even provided a little comic relief. The last third of our book provided some practical guidelines to button up all the hard work we did in year one and some next steps for momentum to keep moving forward.

If you are reading this book soon after a loss, I am so glad it could be here for you. I truly wrote this book to try to be there, right next to you, helping you along the way and guiding you through. I hope that moving forward, the videos and links provide a reliable "go-to" spot for you to find answers.

Any suggestions for something else to post that you think might be helpful, please let me know. Need something more than this book or the resources that can help you? Please don't hesitate to reach out to me or my team directly at hello@donnajeankendrick.com. We will do our best to point you in the right direction.

In closing, as my Babci would say, "I give you peace, love, and a hug to carry you through the day."

GLOSSARY

ASSETS

An asset is any resource of value, tangible or intangible, that is owned by an individual, a company, or a government with the expectation that it will provide an economic benefit. This would be things like your house, rental property, retirement savings accounts, art, stocks, etc. Link to a guide on assets and liabilities: https://www.thebalance.com/a-guide-to-assets-and-liabilities-5197387

BONDS

A bond is a fixed-income instrument that represents a loan made by an investor to a borrower (typically corporate or governmental). It could be thought of as an I.O.U. between the lender and borrower, which includes the details of the loan and its payments. Companies, municipalities, states, and sovereign governments use bonds to finance projects and operations. Bond owners are debtholders, or creditors, of the issuer.

CASH RESERVE

Funds should be set aside for use in emergency situations, the unexpected. For single-income families, the goal is six months of expected costs. For reliable two-income families, the goal is three months of costs. Cash reserves should be kept in liquid accounts such as savings, money markets, or CDs.

On the morning of my wedding day to Greg, my aunt pulled me aside before walking down the aisle. She asked me if I had a secret account, an account that Greg didn't know about, that I could put a percentage of each paycheck into, from both his and my paycheck, so that if there was an emergency, the money could be there. My uncle was a blue-collar worker in Philadelphia at the sugar plant, and when it closed down, she used the funds from that secret account to feed their five kids and pay the mortgage. In my practice, currently, I call this your cash reserve or rainy day fund. And the answer is yes. Yes, I did have that account, and it covered the mortgage for the first two months after Greg's loss. And yes, when my aunt walked through the visitation line before Greg's funeral service, she checked in to make sure I had my rainy day fund ready to go.

COBRA
The Consolidated Omnibus Budget Reconciliation Act (COBRA) gives workers and their families who lose their health benefits the right to choose to continue group health benefits provided by their group health plan for limited periods of time under certain circumstances such as voluntary or involuntary job loss, reduction in the hours worked, transition between jobs, death, divorce, and other life events. Qualified individuals may be required to pay the entire premium for coverage up to 102% of the cost of the plan.

COMMISSIONS
Typically, a commission is compensation for buying or selling a financial asset, such as a stock.

CONFLICTS OF INTEREST

When an advisor's interests (including the interests of their firm) are adverse to the advisor's duty to the client, or when an advisor has duties to one client that are adverse to another client.

EQUITIES

Equity is the portion of a business or other asset that belongs to its owners. It is calculated by taking the total value of the asset and subtracting any outstanding liabilities, like bills and taxes. It can be found on most companies' balance sheets and is used to determine their health. Equity can be split among multiple owners, the same way big companies often have many shareholders. Most of your investments that you want to grow will be in equities, and there are many different types, for example, Large Cap Value, Large Cap Growth, Small Cap, International, and Emerging Markets. During your investment portfolio review, as your financial profession, to help you understand asset classes and the role equities play.

EXCHANGE-TRADED FUNDS (ETF)

An exchange-traded fund, or ETF, is a fund that can be traded on an exchange like a stock, meaning it can be bought and sold throughout the day. ETFs often have lower fees than other types of funds.

Depending on the type, ETFs have varying levels of risk. ETFs can sometimes look and feel like mutual funds but are used differently within your portfolio, either to lower costs, model an index, or help with tactical opportunities. Your financial professional should share the role an ETF plays in the portfolio they are managing for you.

FEES

There are different types of fees that a financial advisor might charge: You may pay a fee based on a percentage of the investable assets the financial advisor manages for you. You may pay an hourly rate or a fixed fee for the service. You may also be able to pay a monthly or quarterly retainer fee (also known as a subscription fee) for the services of a CFP® professional on an ongoing basis.

FINANCIAL PLAN

The output of a collaborative process between client and advisor helps maximize a client's potential for meeting their individual life goals. The plan provides financial advice that integrates relevant elements of the client's personal and financial circumstances.

FIXED INCOME

An income from a pension or investment that is set at a particular figure and does not vary (as a dividend) or rise with the rate of inflation.

INVESTABLE ASSETS

Liquid and near-liquid assets include cash, checking and savings accounts, stocks, bonds, and mutual funds, and retirement accounts, and trusts. Some advisors earn fees based on a percentage of the investable assets they manage for you.

LIABILITIES

Broadly speaking, liabilities are things like credit card debts, mortgages, and personal loans. A liability is a debt you must pay off, now or in the future. Link to a guide on assets and liabilities: https://www.thebalance.com/a-guide-to-assets-and-liabilities-5197387

NET WORTH

Net worth is a measure of wealth. It is the sum of all assets owned by a person or a company minus any obligations or liabilities.

MUTUAL FUND

A mutual fund is a type of financial vehicle made up of a pool of money collected from many investors to invest in securities like stocks, bonds, money market instruments, and other assets. Mutual funds are operated by professional money managers, who allocate the fund's assets and attempt to produce capital gains or income for the fund's investors. A mutual fund's portfolio is structured and maintained to match the investment objectives stated in its prospectus.

NONQUALIFIED

Non-qualified investments are accounts that do not receive preferential tax treatment. You can invest as much or as little as you want in any given year and withdraw at any time. Money that you invest into a non-qualified account is money that you've already received through income sources and paid income tax on.

PROBATE

Probate is the legal process of reviewing a will to determine whether it is valid and authentic. It also refers to the general administration of a deceased person's will or the estate of a deceased person without a will.

QUALIFIED FUNDS

Qualified money refers to money in retirement accounts, such as IRAs, 401(k)s, and 403(b)s. ERISA, or the Employee Retirement Income Security Act, invented qualified money. Before 1974, the only retirement accounts that existed were pensions.

RESTRICTED STOCK UNITS (RSU)

Restricted stock units (RSUs) refer to an agreement by a company to issue an employee shares of stock or the cash value of shares of stock on a future date. Each unit represents one share of stock or the cash value of one share of stock that the employee will receive in the future.

STOCKS

A stock (also known as equity) is a security that represents the ownership of a fraction of a corporation. This entitles the owner of the stock to a proportion of the corporation's assets and profits equal to how much stock they own. Units of stock are called "shares."

TAX-DEFERRED

Tax-deferred status refers to investment earnings that accumulate tax-free until the investor constructively receives the gain, Such as Traditional IRA savings or 401(k) contributions.

TAX-FREE

Tax-free refers to certain types of goods and financial securities (such as municipal bonds) that are not taxed. The tax-free status of these goods, investments, and income may incentivize individuals and business entities to increase spending or investing, resulting in economic stimulus (e.g., ROTH IRA).

RESOURCES

NAVIGATING WIDOWHOOD CAN FEEL OVERWHELMING, BUT you don't have to do it alone. I've compiled a collection of essential resources designed to support and guide you through the first three years of this journey. Download these resources anytime at www.DonnaJeanKendrick.com/Eooks, and remember, you are stronger than you think.

You can enhance your journey with the companion workbook to *A Guide to Widowhood: Navigating the First Three Years*, available now on Amazon, offering practical exercises and additional support as you navigate this challenging time.

OTHER EXTERNAL RESOURCES

- **Credit Review:** www.annualcreditreport.com
- **Grief Recovery:** https://www.griefrecoverymethod.com/
- **Meal Train:** www.mealtrain.com
- **Invest in Others:** www.investinothers.org/abington-health-foundation-grants-for-good-winner/

ABOUT THE AUTHOR

Photo credit: Sarah Miller

Donna Jean Kendrick, founder of Sephton Financial, is not only a financial professional focused on supporting families in transition —whether through widowhood, divorce, or blending families—because she knows first-hand that tomorrow could be quite different from today.

When she was forty years old and had three young children, she experienced one of the worst moments of her life when her first husband, Greg, died suddenly, leaving her to untangle their financial situation while simultaneously grieving and supporting her children through their sorrow.

It was through this experience that she found her calling: supporting other families through transitions so they can breathe easier knowing they're financially secure. In *A Guide for Widowhood*, Donna walks widows and widowers step-by-step through practical matters, like gathering necessary documents, planning a funeral, creating a financial plan, and building a reimagined life. This is Donna's first book. Learn more at www.DonnaJeanKendrick.com.

ABOUT THE PUBLISHER

Founded in 2019, Highlander Press is a vibrant, mid-sized publishing house dedicated to transforming the world through the power of words. We are deeply committed to diversity and bringing big ideas to the forefront. At Highlander Press, we help authors navigate the journey from initial concept through writing, editing, and publishing, culminating in the release of a book that not only fulfills a lifelong dream but also solidifies their expertise and boosts their confidence.

Our unique approach centers on forging strong, collaborative relationships with women-owned businesses across the publishing spectrum, including graphic design, marketing, launching, copyright management, and publicity. We believe in the power of community and operate by the mantra, "a rising tide lifts all boats." This philosophy not only enhances our business model but also ensures that our authors receive unparalleled support and opportunities to succeed.

Join us in making a mark in the literary world, where your voice is heard, and your message has the power to change lives. Visit us at highlanderpressbooks.com to start your publishing journey.

www.ingramcontent.com/pod-product-compliance
Lightning Source LLC
Chambersburg PA
CBHW051629120626
46551CB00014B/1997